Professor Fran … Cyber-
netics at Brun … reau of
Information Sc … ool and
at Sidney Suss … e Moral
Science Tripos … with a
'double first'.

He is the auth … books, the best known of which are *The Brain as a Computer*, *Computers, Science and Society* and *Science and the Crisis in Society*, and has also published a large number of papers. He is a Consultant to NATO and various government departments and is Chairman of the Institution of Computer Science. He is married and has two daughters.

Frank George

Man the Machine

Rightly to be great
Is not to stir without great argument,
But greatly to find quarrel in a straw
When honour's at the stake.
Hamlet, IV, iv

PALADIN
GRANADA PUBLISHING
London Toronto Sydney New York

Published by Granada Publishing Limited
in Paladin Books 1979

ISBN 0 586 08281 6

A Paladin Original

Granada Publishing Limited
Frogmore, St Albans, Herts AL2 2NF
and
3 Upper James Street, London W1R 4BP
1221 Avenue of the Americas, New York, NY 10020, USA
117 York Street, Sydney, NSW 2000, Australia
100 Skyway Avenue, Toronto, Ontario, Canada M9W 3A6
110 Northpark Centre, 2193 Johannesburg, South Africa
CML Centre, Queen & Wyndham, Auckland 1, New Zealand

Made and printed in Great Britain by
Cox & Wyman Ltd, London, Reading and Fakenham
Set in Monotype Ehrhardt

Contents

Preface 7
Argument 9
1 The Crux of the Matter 11
2 Seeing Is Believing 27
3 Machine Thinking 43
4 Language 67
5 The Machine as Scientist 89
6 Emotional Machines 111
7 Creative Machines 121
8 Automation and Cybernation 133
9 Reproduction and the Driving Forces 155
10 Evolving Machine Society 171
11 What It's All About 185
Further Reading 197
Index 201

Preface

This book has been an unusually pleasurable one to write, but also unusually difficult.

The pleasure stems from the fact that I have been working and writing on the subject of cybernetics or machine intelligence for more years than I care to think about, and as a result I feel able to sit down and describe the whole matter from start to finish in one fell swoop. It is not very often in life one has the pleasure of telling a complete and familiar story with the feeling that one has at last got it all clear. This may sound conceited or egotistical but it is not meant to be so. I know what I have to say – right or wrong – and I know that I am saying it believing it to be right.

One difficulty arises through 'jargon'. It is so easy to slip into the habit of talking in the technical terms which are so familiar to me that I have to remind myself constantly that they are not everyday terms. There are other little moments of embarrassment, as I know from talking to my children, such as the effects the word 'algebra' conjures up, which are for some 'all the tortures of the damned'. I did feel the need to introduce Boolean algebra and as a part of my defence I have kept the reference very, very brief. Indeed, at the back of my mind I thought it might prove to be fun for some readers, perhaps giving them fun from mathematics for the first time in their lives. There was also a difficulty over writing clearly without, as my wife put it, 'sounding too remote from reality'. I hope this has been sufficiently achieved, although the subject is quite complicated and it is not always easy to distinguish between what has already been done and what could be done.

For the rest, the story speaks for itself, with not least the implications for society. I have tried to discuss these matters –

these social matters – elsewhere. Early in 1977 I published *Machine Takeover* (Pergamon Press) and *Cybernetics – Science of the Environment* (Elek), developing the story of the social dangers in the first case and giving a brief general picture of the social and philosophical implications in the second. Neither of these previous books did what this one is trying to do – give a straightforward description of the whole process of building the new machine species in terms that are, hopefully, as easy to understand as the subject matter allows. I would like to say a word of special acknowledgment to my wife, Jacqueline, my secretary and elder daughter Mrs Clare Smith, and my secretary at Brunel University, Mrs Pauline Kilbride. All of them have helped in the proof-reading and the typing of the manuscript, but as is usual in these circumstances, I have to absolve them from any responsibility for the final text. I would like also to thank Mr Frank Dale of the BBC whose model, Cedric, I have used for explanatory purposes and over which we worked together to make a television programme of this same story.

I would also like to express my appreciation of the help given by various members of the academic staff of the University of Calgary, the University of Alberta at Edmonton and the Canadian Broadcasting Corporation who have listened to many aspects of the text of this book and made many constructive comments which I have in the main tried to incorporate.

That the book contains a warning is evident. All science – all power – can be used for good or bad, and science is enormously powerful. If such power falls into the wrong hands it can 'corrupt absolutely', and that is what I very much fear may happen. Living in a Britain today that is becoming markedly more totalitarian, one can only fear for the future as power, through specialization, becomes more and more available to the very few. Should that 'very few' eventually turn out to be our government or one or two of our other 'governing bodies' – no prizes are offered for guessing who I have in mind – then God help us!

In the meantime I would like to think this book makes clear and interesting reading and tells a story of scientific success that is still unfolding and *could* enormously benefit mankind.

Beaconsfield 1977 — Frank George

Argument

The main argument of this book is concerned with showing, from various points of view, that machines which behave like men can be 'manufactured' and that they can in the end set up their own machine-controlled society.

A man is himself a sort of machine: we can analyse him with a view to building up a blueprint for him. It will be appreciated that he is a very unusual machine, unlike an aircraft or a motor car, in that he has evolved, and was not manufactured *from* a blueprint (except, of course, that the genes from his parents *are* his blueprint in an obvious sense). We therefore reverse the usual process as we might when we capture an enemy aircraft: we reconstruct the blueprint from the product. Society in turn reflects the nature of man and the organizations which are essential to his survival and yet a threat to his liberty.

The blueprint so far drawn up for human beings *and society* sets out mechanisms – heart and the blood-supply with oxygen added by the lungs and pumped out to the cells of the body, then back again through the veins to the heart for more oxygen. This is much like the supply of oil needed in a car to ensure that all parts are lubricated for proper working. As petrol is needed in a car to work the engine and provide the drive, so food is needed by man in exactly the same way. There are other things besides – electrical circuits for lights and the like, air-conditioning, water-cooling, brakes, springs, etc; or pancreas, liver, lymph glands, kidneys, etc: two systems which both work mechanically.

So we can supply much of what is needed for a blueprint for human beings and therefore for their machine equivalent and the machine society which follows. Notice now that we do not necessarily require *all* the details, since given the starting blueprint for a collection of machines, they will themselves evolve and create their own society. They can, as I shall show, construct themselves much as a human species has offspring, and then create their own protective society.

Many people will throw up their hands in despair at this point and say 'we can never carry through in practice such a complicated matter.' But this is exactly where science is leading us. Unfortunately, many scientists do not appreciate that this is gradually emerging as one of the major end-results of all science and technology.

We have, in this pilgrimage, to keep an eye on people all the time. *The great temptation is to say 'machines can't do this or can't do that', and forget that people can't either.* What, after all, are what we call free will, creative ability and imagination: can you be sure these exist in people, and, if they do, are you sure that they cannot be among the attributes of a machine? It is clear that 'what can be done once, can be done again' and perhaps done better.

This book is intended to show precisely how it will be done, as well as to draw attention to some of the attendant dangers.

1 The Crux of the Matter

There is a label on a cage at a
certain zoo that states simply,
'This animal is new to science.'

Desmond Morris, *The Naked Ape*

Today we are confronted with one of the most intriguing problems ever faced by Man. It is that we seem to be moving towards the point where we can manufacture human beings artificially. This may, at first sight, seem silly, because we know that through the ordinary biological process of copulation man can reproduce himself. The traditional method involves seeds that become fertilized and grow in our ordinary environment into human beings. Why then, we might ask, should anyone want to do in some other way what we know perfectly well how to do by existing means? It may seem pointless.

In fact, far from being pointless, it is a development more important and also more dangerous than either the development of nuclear energy or the problems of the pollution of our environment.

If we can make man in the laboratory, then we can and will first make man in machine form – and we can use wheels instead of legs, and other modifications according to how we decide to use such 'robots' or 'automata'.

There are dangers already with computers, since their ability to collect data in huge banks and process such data (about our taxes, health, credit worthiness, criminal record, etc) at enormously high speeds can be a threat to society. What seems at first sight nothing but a good slave tool for society's more efficient working, turns out also to be a weapon for encouraging an undue amount of surveillance and control. If, like a nuclear bomb, such power gets into the wrong hands, our whole 'democratic' future is in the balance.

The machine 'species' which will arise directly from man is based precisely on the future development of the same computers that provide the existing and fast-increasing number of data banks. That such a machine species might conceivably replace us is obvious. But before we come to any conclusions about the terrible dangers and their attendant moral problems, we must consider the emergence of machine man.

The problem is one of practical skill in translating into reality the theory of how we construct men or construct artificial men. It does not mean that we shall be manufacturing organic man machines; metal and electronic components will be used. But the machines will work like humans and eventually like super-humans. The debate first arises at the theoretical level as to whether such a thing is possible.

One way of putting the key question is: 'Could machines be made to think?' If the answer is yes, it is thought to be obvious that all the rest would be comparatively easy. Man machines could easily be made *less* efficient, less rational and more emotional, to bring them into line with human beings – and for this, something like alarm systems similar to the emotions in man are clearly the very minimum requirements necessary. Since the aim is not to copy human fabrics in our manufacturing process, there is no need to worry about all the complicated chemistry necessary to make muscles, bones and internal organs of one kind or another. While the aim is not to copy (at least initially), it is certainly sensible – even vital – to look hard at human beings and at the basic question about machines thinking. We are bound to proceed by asking ourselves how we learn, think, solve problems and make decisions.

We are concerned with building by metallic and electronic means a system or model which has the same range of capacities that human beings have. The system does not grow to humanlike maturity but is manufactured in the 'adult' stage. We accept there are some dissimilarities which must result from these two major differences between our humanlike machine and human beings, but we will argue that, according to how we construct it, there need be no difference in the capacities and abilities of the finished product.

I should issue a word of warning about the word 'machine'. We obviously do not mean a machine in the sense of a shovel, pneumatic drill, motor car or aircraft. Such machines as these do not think, since in each case a human being uses them and thinks for them. By 'machine', therefore, we mean a system of a very flexible kind which is made in the laboratory and thinks for itself. An aircraft, for instance, which flew itself and made up its own routes, timetables and the like, would certainly think – whatever definition is adopted for thinking. Of all the machines we have mentioned, the present jumbo jet comes nearest to a 'thinking' aircraft, as almost every part of the complete flight is performed automatically.

I should also perhaps say right at the start that there are a number of words which will be used and about which we have to be very wary. We talk of 'consciousness', 'awareness', 'creativity' and 'emotions', and in each case we use the words as we do in the case of humans, at least as far as we can tell. But we need to explain, as we deal with each example, the only tests available to us which help us to decide whether or not machines can (or even need to) possess such human capacities.

Most of the experimental work in the field of 'artificial intelligence' is carried out on computers, and there is a good reason for this: computers are easily the largest machines available for modelling purposes. One could in theory have started to build a robot by gradually fitting together the necessary bits and pieces empirically, but it would, in practice, be wholly uneconomical in terms both of money and of time. Bear in mind also that a computer is incomplete. It is a vehicle which is completed only by the inclusion of the computer program which tells it what to do. This again is like an aircraft which requires a pilot. Now the feeling still exists among many people that since a human being writes the program, the control is in the end really vested in him.

The answer to this is that the programmer only starts the process off, by telling the computer how to collect information and formulate generalizations and the like, and not *what* information to collect; and he does not interfere with the computer after it takes up its own independent existence. The important point about this is that in almost all existing computer installations the programmer does in fact set out all the instructions – this is the program – and the computer carries them through. Even here there are conditional instructions, but they do not offer the computer any escape from what the programmer has set out. It escapes, much as a child escapes from his parents, when it is allowed independent interaction with the outside world. This part of the progression is quite essential, and in fact, whenever we wonder about the new machine offspring, we can think of them as being like children.

The extent to which they can be controlled once they have their wings and can fly on their own, is one of the great problems we, who manufacture such machines, have to consider.

The machine man, as planned, is built 'mature' and does not therefore have any growth problems, as I have already mentioned. The human child has to develop his nerve connections at the same time as his body grows and he is gathering his experience. That problem will be encountered when we go for man-made seeds which grow into embryos and then children and so on to adulthood. But as long as the readymade man-machine (robot) is the object of the exercise we can proceed to the fully developed machine and leave it to acquire its own experience, and this of course will take time.

To put the matter at the simplest level and to give a preview of the mode of thought to be pursued, look at a machine playing a game. If we make it an easy game like noughts-and-crosses (call it OAX for short), we can see how the machine learns to play it. The game is easy to play and it can be approached by numbering the squares like this:

8	1	6
3	5	7
4	9	2

This 'magic square' technique makes OAX also easy to describe, because the player who first fills up a set of three numbered squares which add up to 15, wins. This clearly depicts OAX. We now find that all our man-machine needs to do to learn how to play OAX is to keep in store number-sequences such as

5 8 6 4 1 3 L
5 1 3 8 7 W
5 4 6 8 3 2 9 7 1 D
5 4 6 8 3 2 9 1 7 W
and so on,

where W is won, L is lost and D is drawn, as seen from the point of view of the starting player. The machine keeps a record of games won, lost and drawn, and gradually 'learns' only to make moves that are followed by W. This way it eliminates all errors and never loses. If it plays against a player who has also learned to play perfectly, every game is then, at best, drawn, so it will have to settle for D instead of W. The main thing is to avoid L.

The interesting point to notice is that it needs only to keep a fairly simple record and that record is made up of who moves where (the two players of course move alternately) and what the result was. This means that it has a store which is composed of many sequences, although it would collect only those it has actually met. The whole possible number is too great and would waste storage space since most of the possible games will never actually be played. The test piece is simply to weigh the best moves positively and the worst moves negatively after the game is over. This weighing is done simply by using a pair of numbers (m, n) and adding 1 to n for every game played and 1 to m only if the game is not lost, and then choosing the highest relevant fraction m/n for any move made.

In the second of the earlier examples,

5 1 3 8 7 W

we look at the table which starts

51 and 5138

and add 1 to both m and n for each of them. If 51 had m = 13, n = 20 and 5138 had m = 8, n = 8 associated with them, these would become (14, 21) and (9, 9) respectively. Then next time a game started 51, we would look at the various possibilities, 512, 513, 514, 516, 517, 518, 519, and choose the move, 2, 3, 4, 6, 7, 8 or 9 which had the largest fraction m/n associated with it. By this method m/n fractions associated with the 'bad moves' cannot increase, and the m/n fraction for the 'good moves' can and do, so in the end we must learn, at least not to lose.

This is an example of reinforcement, sometimes called the Law of Effect, and, where emotions are involved, it has been called the pleasure-pain principle. Where something is done which satisfies, it is repeated, and vice versa. To win therefore *must* satisfy, either by some emotional state or by building in a rule which is the equivalent.

If OAX were a longer game like chess, our machine would have to break the game up into sections, since otherwise too many good moves might be abandoned merely because the game was ultimately lost, and indeed too many bad moves might be preserved even though the game was won. This would make learning a very long and difficult process.

But although the next step is to generalize on these results and apply them to other games and show how learning those other games is thereby speeded up, we are anticipating too much of the story too quickly. I shall return to our general thesis that machines can be made to think, and ask why anyone should believe it to be impossible (which is what many people do believe).

The first objection is a religious one. It argues that man was made by God and that man is unique, for if another manlike system were to be manufactured, it could only be by God. This is not, it seems to me, a valid objection, since there is no reason why man, given 'free will', should not exercise his genius to such ends. He has certainly often done far worse with his skills. A number of people with religious convictions work in these fields of cybernetics and artificial intelligence and do not hold such a view. Of course, if you do not believe in God anyway, then the argument becomes irrelevant.

The second objection is compounded of horror and a sense of inconvenience, born of a sort of jealousy. This is not to be taken seriously at the intellectual level, but could be a very effective obstacle in practice. Merely being inconvenient or horrid is clearly irrelevant to the truth or otherwise of events or propositions, and since few people would argue seriously against even the possibility of the emergence of a rival biological species, it is not easy to see how there can be any substance in this form of argument. An alternative 'mechanical' species is clearly a logical *possibility*, however inconvenient.

A third objection is really based on the idea that you may be able to make a machine think in a 'cold logical' way, but it could never be made to encompass human thinking with all its complicated overtones. I shall attempt to deal with this objection later by considering, in separate chapters, emotion and creativity. But there is no reason for supporting such an objection, since the emotions and the creative skills – these to some extent must go together – are perfectly capable of being reproduced artificially. What starts out as a sort of emergency fuse system can become a complicated alarm system and then a full emotional system to create pleasure and pain to go with certain (perhaps all) actions. Whenever a part of our robot is threatened, it can register a state so unpleasant – by interference with its storage registers and the like – that it tries to avoid it. Sensors built for the purpose are necessary, but nothing mysterious is involved: no more, anyway, than is involved in thinking. I shall say more on this matter later.

A fourth objection is a mathematical one and somewhat complicated. It says in effect that a system of considerable complexity and precisely defined cannot be shown to be both completely defined and wholly consistent at the same time. In effect this means that highly precise systems such as machines cannot be self-sufficient. This is not so, though, because the real problem is not one of self-sufficiency or of being consistent and well-defined, but one of *showing* this to be the case. The same problem applies to human beings; they cannot show themselves to be self-sufficient or complete by any precise argument, because the price of precision is to go beyond the system, to something imprecise. A single example may help. If asked to define a term in language or explain a process, we necessarily use other words. These other words then need to be defined or explained and the words used in the definitions and explanations are themselves in need of definition and explanation. It is clear that sooner or later something has to be taken for granted and this is as much a problem for a human being as it is for a machine. Any sort of *description*, in precise terms, of a system is either self-referential or in part outside the system itself: in fact it always has to have some aspects outside the system.

The fifth and final objection we shall consider is that a machine does only what it is made to do or, to use computer terms, a computer does only what it is programmed to do. The reason this is false is because you can, and must, program a computer to program itself if you are to produce a thinking machine. The same problem applies to children. If they did only what they were programmed to do, then they would never acquire the ability to think and learn for themselves. It is often said that Lady Lovelace, a friend of Charles Babbage the great computer pioneer, was the first person who gave voice to this last objection, and perhaps it is the most telling objection to machine intelligence. It is one that would hold water if it were not that machines can in fact be given that essential independence which allows them not only the ability to perform certain actions, but to learn to perform these actions for themselves. The programmer only initiates their activity (like parents and their children) and gives them 'free will' to pursue whatever ends they choose.

The counter argument against all these arguments is only complete when the actual task is carried through, but in the meantime we can at least say that there is no reason to accept any of the arguments put forward so far as to why a manlike system ('machine') cannot be artificially constructed. Of course, if anyone can supply new evidence to support their beliefs (or disbeliefs), then we shall always be prepared to listen, but in the meantime we shall continue to pursue the objective.

The major psychological block that most people have is in the imagination. It is not easy to realize that human beings need not have looked like human beings, because to be intelligent, or indeed emotional, does not require that you *look like* a human being. It is even more difficult to imagine a machine, complete with dials, switches and flickering lights, to have consciousness; but why should it not? Consider how you would set about convincing somebody that for a machine to have consciousness is impossible. The fact is that there is absolutely no reason, nor any evidence, which tells us that human beings are the only creatures (or systems) which have these properties.

Leave aside the problem of the imagination and ask yourself

the question: what will be the effect of having living machines? These machines will be designed by us and built by us, at least in the first place. Later, they will learn to build themselves, just as they will learn a whole lot of other things besides.

The point to note here is that we already use machines to make machines, and increasingly these are automated so that the whole process is probably, in the modern automated factory, man-independent. If this is followed by showing that our man-machine, which is intelligent and can be autonomous, can also reproduce itself, then the possibility of the evolution of an independent species is clear. Such a demonstration has been made and will be discussed later, but in any case it is clearly presaged by the very existence of automated machine manufacture. One can see here the obvious possibility of the direct utilization of raw materials by machines working on their own initiative.

The effect of all this on society could plainly be dramatic. Should we build such machines, since they might dominate or even eliminate us? Look again at the question of intelligence. Suppose that to be intelligent requires that a system purposively collects data which it can sense in its environment. It sorts, classifies and files away this data. It draws logical conclusions and generalizations from it and uses them to control its environment (much as a scientist does, for example) and especially to satisfy its needs – especially those which contribute to its survival. Then, granted that it can do all these things and assuming that this is what all intelligent human beings do (and is what intelligence is about), it is virtually certain that what we have is a superspecies. This follows, simply because our artificial brain is no longer constrained by the size of the human head; it can be as 'big-headed' as we want to make it. Speed will not be a problem either, because we can make it as fast, more or less, as we please.

Digital computers can process mathematical data thousands or millions of times faster than human beings. Similarly, they can be enormously faster at doing anything else. Indeed, to do mathematics and logic is one of the biggest tests of doing anything intelligent. Most problems can be reduced to a logical or mathematical form.

Of course, there are practical as well as moral problems involved. We should build such machines if we can control them and make them work for the good of society. We are able to build them, just as we now build computers which are vast and complicated. But once built, and once they have the capacity to reproduce themselves and the intelligence to control their environment, we can no longer guarantee to control them. The problem then is, should we build them if we cannot control them? Perhaps we should ask the same of having children? We shall return to this issue again more than once before our pilgrimage is complete.

The Lady Lovelace view of machines is that since they do only what they are told, they are slaves. After all, you can always cut off their power supply. You can, as it is so eloquently put, always 'pull out the plug'. I shall discuss most of these points again, but in the last case the simple answer is that the one thing you *cannot* do is pull out the plug. The machine is intelligent enough to stop you. In fact, of course, it could become much more efficient at pulling out our plugs, so to speak. This is the danger to human beings; they could be destroyed by their own 'children'. The same is true, of course, of their own natural children, as some people have learned to their cost.

All innovation tends to be two-edged, as nuclear energy well illustrates, and the two-edged nature of our world of 'artificial intelligence', as it is sometimes called, is fairly clear. But the snag is that you cannot abolish curiosity, since it is such a basic human drive. What you have to achieve is some measure of control, at least of direction.

Why can we not make intelligent machines and limit the extent to which they can control their 'limbs', in the form of wheels, automatic legs and arms, and huge weight-lifters and diggers. To do so is difficult and it becomes very difficult indeed if we decide to build a robot soldier or policeman. A dilemma arises, since it needs enough intelligence to do the job you have given it, but not so much that it can use the degree of independence you have given it to turn upon you.

The humanoid of science fiction is sometimes said to have a prime goal directive which cannot be abrogated. Survival, or possibly sex, are the nearest we get in human beings. If we want, we *can* abrogate these by committing suicide or by being celibate. If we did this as a species, though, the species would die out, and for obvious reasons. Even so, no prime goal directive is such that it cannot be overcome, and that is why, given enough intelligence, we cannot ever be sure that our machine man will be 'safe'.

It is just possible that some suitable control recipe could be drawn up, but the necessary policing, as in the case of nuclear arms, to see that no one breaks the agreement – and that is what it must be – is still virtually impossible.

Privacy is already threatened by our data-bank society, and the threat of totalitarianism in one form or another is already with us. If we cannot contain the present problem of control of control, since this is what it is, then the next problem we meet is that of the machine species and the threat of their takeover.

What we are aiming to do, above all else, is to describe how man is reproduced artificially, or 'as a machine'; how machines can be made to think, and think more logically and more clearly than man. It is all the product of man's genius, but the consequences have to be carefully considered.

Historically, the problem has been tackled in stages and it is reasonable to think of it in much the same way. An artificial human who is readymade, by which one means it is built as an adult, must be able to sense its environment: it needs eyes and ears, at least. It then needs to learn, and this involves the sort of adaptability already discussed. This simple adaptation has then to be made much more complicated. It is not enough to make moves successfully in games. The machines must form the general concepts involved in making moves, and 'realize' that they apply to *any* game. This sort of generalizing process is vital to a 'thinking machine'. The whole undertaking will fail if at the same time the machine does not possess a language, and just as it needs to learn to play games and not merely be told how to play, it must be able to learn a language. If it is simply given one, that is fair enough, but there must be the inbuilt learning capacity, otherwise a changing environment will find it unable to adapt, and it will not survive.

Thinking follows from perception, learning and language and we now have a purposeful, motivated, goal-seeking, problem-solving system which can evolve.

The matter of 'intelligence' is clearly all-important. We are saying that a machine that is goal-directed (regardless of the nature of the goal) and has these capacities to perceive, learn and use language, will automatically have the capacity to be intelligent: the question then is merely one of degree. The degree of intelligence in our man-made machine will be influenced by 'genetics' (how it is designed) and also by its particular experience, since all of this makes sense only if the machine lives in some sort of society, whether machine only or man-and-machine.

More abstruse problems like self-maintenance and reproduction can be discussed later. But at least in the short term the above must be achieved.

The question must be asked: how far have we got, so far? This is what this book is about, apart from the moral problem of appreciating the consequences of success and asking whether these consequences include too great an element of risk.

One last basic question frequently asked in this context of machine manufacture is that of economics and the use of resources. There are various ways in which this matter can be regarded.

First, there is no sign at all that computers are not being produced in great numbers. Already the cost of these computers is being reduced as fast as their effective power increases. If we also bear in mind that the cost of the sort of robots or automata we are considering should be little more than that of existing computers, there is absolutely no reason to suppose an economic or energy problem.

If there is an energy resources problem, then it is likely to be encountered by man far more quickly than it is by our man-machines, since they will not need to exist in vast numbers to exercise their power gained from being organized into a social species. Furthermore, their potential 'immortality', comparable to that of a motor car, could be used as a cheaper method of manufacturing the species than a replacement method.

The possibility of a central 'brain' and remotely controlled limbs further emphasizes the economies that might be utilized; and, finally, if the stage is ever reached of the production of artificial cells that grow, once again the economic problem is at least no worse than that facing humanity. The ease of population control in such a species indeed makes the problem a great deal easier.

There may be economic problems embodied in all scientific research – the nuclear bomb, space flight and so on – but the money has usually been found. In our present case it seems to me, at least on the face of it, that the economic problem is negligible.

2 Seeing Is Believing

The words *is* and *is not*, which imply the agreement or disagreement of two ideas, must exist, explicitly or implicitly, in every assertion.

Augustus de Morgan

We are absolutely serious about constructing a machine-in-evolution or a machine species, and not just a machine. Although the latter requires a great deal of thought and effort, in fact it is by far the major part of the problem. Given the 'thinking machine', the machine species follows easily enough.

We are also really serious about playing the role of God. We will construct a species and give it a 'freedom of will' and then sit back and watch it going its own way, exercising the same efforts to control it as parents do with children: what will result one can only guess at. We shall have to consider carefully when and where to take cover ourselves – this is the trouble. But leaving aside, for the time being, our guesses as to the future, we must look at the way in which our intelligent machine can actually be built.

The process is a progressive one. One starts with simple beginnings and then moves on from them, showing that the basic principles are the same throughout. What changes with the growing complexity is mainly the size of the system, which increases enormously. It is not so much a matter of introducing new principles.

The story begins with simple adaptiveness, as shown by a model we shall call *Cedric*, a maze-running machine or artefact. Maze-runners have been built before, which can either turn right, turn left, turn around, or go straight on at choice points in a maze; but the implications of such systems had not been fully realized. From such apparently simple beginnings enormous complexity can arise, as will be made clear.

Cedric is made up of the absolute minimum of sensory equipment, in the form of two sensors which can register the edge of a line and whether the line turns left or right or comes to an end. The two sensors are on either side of Cedric. It has an electric motor and a battery, also a steering device which allows it to move along and turn, and it has the *built-in* response (like a human or animal instinct) to turn left at each choice-point.

Superimposed on the mechanical linkage is a set of programs, which allow more complex behaviour, whereby Cedric (the 'rat') accepts a reward ('cheese') with 'enough pleasure' to note where the reward was received and how it (Cedric) got there. When a reward is available again, Cedric returns via the known route to the known goal. If the reward is not there, Cedric then proceeds in the 'search mode' to try to find the reward. In doing so it will, according to the nature of the maze, continually override, wherever necessary, its 'instinctive' propensity to turn left.

It is clear now that we can use micro-miniaturized components in our control system, which allow Cedric to store information and provide a working program which it can carry around with it. As the weight of the programming requirement noticeably increases, so there arises a need for Cedric to use a 'remote-controlled brain'. This is an important development.

We are reminded that it is a sort of biological accident that our brain is in our body and contains on the spot all the limbs necessary for transportation and for manipulation of the environment. This has vital consequences later in our story, as we evolve our systems from simple maze-running machines to full-scale thinking machines which first equal and then surpass the human being. The question of 'biological accidents' will arise frequently, so it is as well to make a special note of this concept.

But now we remind ourselves that we must provide our robot with 'limbs' if it is to manipulate the environment, and that is essential to an artificially intelligent machine just as it is to a human being. The 'limbs' can be as remote as we please, even perhaps in the hands of a human being. It is rather like a man who has lost his arms and legs but still has the brain of an Einstein. No harm is done if, when he wants action, he can use someone else's arms and legs.

Why, though, should we bother at all with systems like Cedric? Maze-running machines of one kind or another were built a good thirty years ago. They were all able to proceed up a maze and 'make choices' and reach the goal box. Two important things have happened since those early days. In the first place, a simple maze-runner is now tiny by comparison, or, what amounts to the same thing, for the same size it can do a great deal more. The second point is that it has become clearer all the time that the difference between the control system (the brain) of a maze-runner and the human brain is only a matter of size. This statement will be qualified later, but there is every reason to believe in the essential simplicity of the *principles* involved in the human brain. We can guess that exponential growth in the size of a system is what changes it.

By exponential growth we mean the extraordinary rate at which things can grow and multiply. If you place £1 on a roulette table and lose, and then double your stakes, and continue to do this after each loss, then at the fifteenth bet you are staking £16,384! It is this sort of magnitude that makes the human brain so effective, although we do not know exactly how the human brain works.

What we do know is that a control system which can store the simple information required to run a maze, can grow in its power at just such an enormous rate.

The process is rather like having learned to play a game. The next 'similar' game is far easier to play and the next one even easier, because very general common rules are, in some way, being learned. In other words 'getting started' is the main problem. Once it has begun, the control design can improve its range of activities at an astonishing, even exponential, rate.

In particular, Cedric can learn to find a 'reward' and register (remember) the fact that it is a reward (Cedric gives a 'hoot of pleasure' when it finds it), and can note other things in passing. If Cedric is given two rewards – cheese and water – and given two states, 'hungry' and 'thirsty', then we observe a new level of complexity. If when hungry it discovers water, it continues to search until it finds food, but it nevertheless makes a note of the fact in its memory store, and when thirsty in future it will remember where it will (probably) get water. The word 'probably' is included of course, because the water may still be there: this is true both of life and more obviously of the experimental situation.

The presence or absence of water is a matter of special significance to learning, because it reminds us of the distinction between *learning* and *having learned*. If the environment were fixed and unchanging, then all one would need to do is learn about it, learn the rules of the game as it were, and from then on a decision on what to do in any given situation would be merely a test of memory. But because so much does change, an intelligent adaptable system has to continue, if it is to survive, to learn all the time.

In fact, for an individual, the ratio of learning to 'having learned' generally diminishes with age, precisely because so much has already been learned and so much is in fact unchanging. Here we also glimpse a distinction between learning particularities and learning generalities. In maze-running terms, we could say that most mazes have choice-points. This normally means that you have to go left, go right, go straight on or turn around. Then, although particular mazes may vary in their details, the general principles on which they are constructed are broadly the same. This is a strong clue to human intelligence and how learning grades over into thinking. It does so by going beyond the particular to the general and can then deal in both.

Cedric could be made to 'think' by the imposition of higher-level programs, but this requires – sooner or later – that the brain be remote from the body. This is simply because our artefact's space limitation (power/weight ratio) is such that it cannot carry too much brain with it. The size of the human head is a similar limitation, and is one of the reasons why man's intelligence will eventually be surpassed. In the meantime Cedric relies on remote control to overcome the limitation. The same remote control occurs in some measure in the case of man, where he uses language to communicate with other people so that he can use corporate knowledge, and not merely his individual knowledge. This shows the vital necessity for language, since without this, human beings could not have accumulated information from generation to generation: this cumulative process of acquiring knowledge through language is what Alfred Korzybski called 'time-binding'.

So important is this point that it should be explained here again that the 'biological accident' of the size of the human head limits the size of the human brain. Our man-machine will not be limited in this way, since we can make the brain as large as we like. The human being, through language, utilizes the brain of the species, so that the solutions to the problems of living are shared. This in turn leads to specialization, since none of us knows enough to deal with a whole range of problems. For convenience, and for their own social safety, machines will also be 'individual', and as soon as they are, they will need a language in order to communicate.

There are also the seeds of social organization showing themselves in the notion of 'time-binding' and the need for corporate knowledge, though in some measure we are now anticipating our future discussion. One thing, however, is clear at this point, and that is that the social nature of learning and communication removes the need for each individual to learn everything for himself.

Cedric is to be thought of as a simple maze-running machine with a potential for learning a great deal about its own world and for storing that information, even if at some point it leaves its growing brain behind and operates by remote control.

Super-Cedric, as it (our man-machine) will be called, appears on the scene sooner or later, where the largest possible computer becomes the remote-control 'brain', and the Cedric maze-runner is only one of many limbs that Super-Cedric possesses.

We could, of course, develop the Cedric family in any number of stages. We might start with sub-Cedric, which is a machine that has little or no self-controlling element at all. All cars, most aircraft, etc are sub-Cedric. Then, above Cedric, we can have all sorts of degrees of adaptation, involving more sensors for perception and larger memory stores, until we eventually get to Super-Super-Cedric, and who knows where we might finish.

But again we are getting ahead of our story, since we want to deal at this stage with the input of information and its interpretation – what has usually been called *sensing* and *perceiving*.

In fact, we shall soon see for ourselves that the input of information, the interpreting of that input and the central processing of information grade over from one so-called cognitive capacity to another. All of these processes are energized by the motivational process which provides goals, allowing the needs and the understanding of the systems to be conjoined.

But we can start by concentrating on Cedric's sensors, and

simply say that they are ways of detecting a shade gradient which distinguishes the end of a black area and the beginning of a white one. This means that it can, given the motor of a steering device, track a line and provide information about the behaviour of that line: it turns left, it turns right, it goes straight on or it stops. This is about all Cedric needs to know, except – and this is a generalization which Cedric does not need to make explicit – that goal boxes are where 'food' and 'drink' occur, and are at end-points of the maze. The process of making generalizations explicit will become vital only for Super-Cedric.

In fact, of course, Cedric needs to distinguish food from drink, and has to be able to distinguish its own internal need for food from that for drink, and be 'aware of' the existence of either need. These four factors could be represented quite easily by a simple control system which registers two different 'perceptions' (we could simply represent food by a short flash of light and water by a long flash) and the internal needs could be represented by a switch's being thrown. When there is hunger and the food is found, the switch is thrown back and a hooter can be made to give out the message of pleasure. It can be seen from this that such noises could be the beginnings of a language in a Cedric society.

So much of this capacity for simple but intelligent activity is designed into artefacts, just as instinctive behaviour patterns are *the basis of* (or are designed into) the behaviour of all organisms right up to and including human beings.

We have to superimpose highly flexible learning systems, such as reinforcement or the Law of Effect, upon the pre-wired instinctive patterns. This makes up the beginnings of 'intelligence' and provides the sexual appetite and the need to eat and drink which are characteristic of people, and essential to their survival. According to definitions of survival, we see that systems without such survival characteristics simply could not exist.

All this makes clear that even minimal perceptual processing can entail a high degree of intelligent behaviour. A one-eyed deaf man can do almost everything a normal man can do. This can be taken as a reminder that our perceptual systems provide a very high degree of redundancy. We depend upon this redundancy in identifying our environment with confidence, since it is evidence from more than one of our senses that convinces us that a man has, for example, just kicked a ball: we not only see it but we hear the sound and are perhaps hit by the ball.

Cedric's perceptual processes are minimal, yet they require discriminations, and these discriminations need to be recorded. The sensor needs to be able to differentiate between two states: one is black-to-white and the other is white-to-black. So if a black line is drawn on a white base, then the change-point from black to white means the edge of the line which is being left on the left. If it is white to black, it is being left on the right; then we need to fire off 'move right' to track the line. This is simple, yet but it is the basis of all perceptual activity, and it might be guessed that such a perceptual processor is a classification system (or a set of them) built upon such sensory discriminations.

We must turn now to Super-Cedric and see how the sensing and classification processes develop on a larger scale. We need for the moment to imagine a very large computer acting as our central processor (our brain); and we know that this may not be identical in operation to the human brain, but we also know it can achieve similar results. Any differences will be worried about later. We will not, it will be remembered, be concerned primarily, at least at first, with imitating the detail of the human brain, only its broad approach.

A description must gradually emerge, as it becomes necessary, on a stage-by-stage basis, of the control computer of Super-Cedric. It is composed of a large store (actually two stores: high-speed and central; and slower, but still very fast, and peripheral) and a processor, which actually includes the high-speed store, and performs arithmetical and other operations on basic data which are arithmetical, symbolic and verbal. The set of instructions which operates Super-Cedric is the program. The computer programs can be interactive (they can learn) and the whole system can be made self-programming: all this will gradually emerge in detail as our discussion is broadened to include humanlike thought.

As far as input is concerned, we have to look at our available sensors. In the human being these involve eyes, ears, a tongue, a nose, hands and internal sensors (compare Cedric's knowledge of when it is hungry and thirsty) to tell when he feels movements or detects pain, and also when he is aware of hunger and thirst.

Our man-machine, although not meant at this stage to be a copy (simulation) of man, is built in his image. Super-Cedric's eyes can be the equivalent of a colour-television camera and the ears a radio receiver. Taste, smell and touch have less obvious readymade equivalents, although we can manufacture systems to take care of them.

Now our basic question is simply how best to break down these special senses into discrete states in the control. The 'eye' can be used as a yardstick, and it can be argued that if it can be understood how sight can be simulated, then the other senses – being apparently simpler – should present relatively less problems.

The human eye includes a sensitive layer of nervous tissue called the retina, and this records coloured spots and their movement. The colour effects are chemically achieved, and the whole thing (picture) is encoded and sent to the brain (the computer of Super-Cedric). Human vision is further complicated by 'alarm' connections to other parts of the brain which stimulate fear. These alarm signals must also occur in Cedric in the face of danger. A failure to be alarmed by danger means a failure to survive as an individual, or as a species.

The television camera, rather like the eye, picks up scenes, encodes them and sends them to a film where they are recorded, but more important for our purposes, sends them to a monitor (this is like the visual part of the brain) where the scenes are reproduced. We can, centrally or in the control room, now move the camera to scan the whole scene and all the pictures are picked up. The dots picked up by the human retina are similar to the dots one sees in photographs when they are blown up. The television equivalents are lines.

We manufacture a series of pictures of our surroundings and encode them in such a way as to record a moving scene. We can, of course, now leave the information in coded form and send it straight into the computer or brain. In other words we may not need to reassemble the pictures on a monitor or in the visual part of the brain.

The analogy here is with 'rethinking' an automatic pilot. A robot pilot would not need a visual control panel, as this is just an adaptation to the fact of human eyes; rather, information about height, airspeed and position would be fed directly into the computer part of the control (a pilot version of Super-Cedric). Since eyes are no longer necessary as a link between the necessary information (height etc) and the brain (the control), we can obviously build special-purpose robots in the same way as we have specialists among human beings: doctors, accountants, lawyers; or, to specialize still further, brain specialists, investment specialists, barristers and, most important of all, as we shall see later, scientists. But the main point here is that Super-Cedric can be manufactured to process visual inputs in many different ways, the most obvious being by digital control.

Visual inputs are fed into the *stage one* processing system in the form of collections of dots or segments of lines. Remember, from geometry, that a line is just a set of dots. Next it must be noted that objects in the loosest sense include men, dogs, chairs, guns, sheets of paper, puffs of smoke and everything from the relatively permanent to the extremely transient, and all are composed visually of these dot sets.

A man is not necessarily recognized immediately from his dot set, but from a second set that fills in gaps and smoothes curves, rather as one can imagine the complete picture from a partly finished jigsaw puzzle. In fact, the processes of classification now require not just two stages but many. But before making this point clear I shall describe the basic concept of classification.

To illustrate the principle of classification in a very simple case: if we have four elements labelled A, B, C and D, we can classify them singly (four classes), in pairs AB, AC, AD, BC, BD, CD (six of these), in triplets ABC, ABD, BCD, ACD (four of these) and all four ABCD. This sort of classification in mathematics is called a combination; and if all possible orders are considered, it is called a permutation. Such classifications can now take a slightly different form. If we have elements a, b, c, d, e, f, then we can say a, b and c belong to X; d and e belong to Y; and f belongs to Z. These are sets of classes in mathematical terms, and it is the last word, 'class', that gives its name to the process of classification.

The next stage is to consider all possible characteristics of our world – blue, green, round, small, etc – and consider all possible ways of classifying them. If there are N such characteristics, then there are $2^N - 1$ classifications. This can become very large, since $2^N = 16,384$ when $N = 14$ and there are therefore 16,383 classifications. So although our sensory systems can work on the basis of classification, we are going to have troubles with the size of the system unless we are careful.

We can say next that an object has two legs, two arms, two eyes, one nose, etc. An infinite number of different properties can be enumerated as our probes become finer and finer, but long before we have gone very far we say that it is a man and it is a particular man called Charlie Smith. The final identification is a higher-level classification, but the lowest visual level, involves a combination of observed characteristics. When a person is very familiar, only a few characteristics may be needed to identify him. When he is wholly unfamiliar, you may recognize that he is a man but you do not know him. We should say straight away that *the context* in which the object (say, Charlie Smith) occurs – and this is something at a higher level – is a principal factor in performing the recognition.

The reason for levels of classification is partly concerned with the size of the necessary sensory system. If N gets big quickly, the necessary detecting elements must also get big quickly. By classifying (detecting) in stages, we cut down the need for such huge classification systems. This need is further cut down because one does not need to sense *all* the characteristics of a man to know he is a man, and many combinations possible in a classification system do not, in any case, occur in reality.

Granted, then, that our camera picks up coloured dot sets and encodes them as pulse trains, it then fires them into the control system of Super-Cedric, who goes through the visual analysis of the properties and says 'Charlie Smith'. In fact, it gets information also from other sources, such as the smell of after-shave and the sound of a familiar West of England accent, even supposing the subject is not allowed to say, 'You will remember me, I'm Charlie Smith.'

The *second level* of classification is where all the different sensory pieces are put together, as it were, to define the whole scene.

Memory clearly now plays a vital part because these sensory sets, and combinations of them, are compared with those previously encountered and they are then identified. They are identified partly by each individual sense and partly on account of the total picture where all the pieces fit together consistently. Memory also includes the vital temporal context, since we know that Charlie Smith lives in Kansas City and that he drinks in the Democratic Club. We know he is one of the few people we are likely to know there and we have just arrived and have gone straight to that club, so we find identification that much easier precisely because it is expected. The dangers here, and the embarrassment caused by false identification, are well known.

We say, in human terms, that we expected to see him, and if we had arranged the meeting we would be very surprised if we did not see him. But as it is, although we had not arranged it, we are half expecting it. There is no need to labour the point that what we expect to happen quite dramatically influences our perceptions. Our man-machine works on the same principle of classification.

There are, of course, a number of wrinkles that need ironing out. People (and machines too) do not need, as I have said already, to see all aspects of a person in order to recognize him. More often than not a nose alone would do and certainly a face is almost always sufficient. This means the recognition process is greatly speeded up by a sampling process, and the great redundancy made available by continued inspection (like an expert archaeologist looking at a specimen) is needed only for the very fine and delicate sorts of recognition process.

Recognition has been discussed as if it were the bulk of perception, which it is, but the perception of something not previously seen requires the setting up of a new model of the object made up of new sensory dot sets. These new sets can be broadly classified already as man, cat, mirror, etc, but we now elaborate the (small) differences which occur with the similarities allowing us to identify Harry Smith (never met before) or a valuable Persian cat (also a newcomer).

One thing stands out from all this, and it is that our artefact (Cedric), in simply tracking lines and finding food, is doing nothing different *in principle* from our man-machine (Super-Cedric), or human beings, meeting people in the Kansas City Democratic Club for a lunch-time Martini. The differences *in practice* are differences in the complexity of the objects or events to be identified (recognized, perceived, etc) and therefore the size of the identifying system and memory store required. The very interesting question of language, which certainly complicates the whole picture, is yet to be considered. But we can at least see in Cedric's present silent world the processes in broad terms that can allow an artificially constructed system (which can loosely be called a machine) like Super-Cedric to go about the process of providing input and a great deal of internal processing.

It is because of the vast increase in internal processing that we need brains working on remote control, as humans do in effect by using language and living in societies. Again we see the specialization arising among people and the need for accumulation of knowledge from generation to generation. These both depend on language: we now enlist the whole society, providing a sort of collective brain. This collective brain could never belong to any one person; similarly, in a machine, it cannot, as it gets larger and larger, be 'humped' around, nor is there any need.

There is one further point which should be made, and made with emphasis. There exist, in reality, all the components which go to make up both Cedric and Super-Cedric. The former exists now and can be observed doing its job, the latter also exists but is still what might be called a 'mock-up' in a laboratory. What is required for Super-Cedric is a large computer with a huge auxiliary store; special-purpose inputs, like optical recognition systems; the usual paraphernalia of ordinary computers and moving limbs such as are currently seen in automation and used by the medical world in supplying artificial limbs. Cedric itself, or a whole set of Cedrics, as well as the auxiliary limbs, can be remotely controlled by Super-Cedric. It should be noted that this is not some remote 'pipe dream', but something happening here and now.

Super-Cedric's other major requirement is a matter of software, which means the complex programs which operate it. This requires special techniques such as those called *heuristics*.

I can best describe *heuristics* by contrasting them with *algorithms*. An algorithm is a strict and precise procedure, like a proof in mathematics. If I wanted to know how many people were on the telephone in Los Angeles I could look through the directory and write 1 against the first, 2 against the second, 3 against the third and so on, and the largest number would give me the answer, at least to the number of names in the directory. By contrast, a heuristic is a rough guide or approximation. I would flick over the pages of the directory and say 'about 4 million'.

Heuristic methods play a vital part in moving over from the behaviour of simple artefacts to man-machines. Most of human thinking is a mixture of algorithms and heuristics, principally the latter.

One last comment, and that is on a matter which will come up from time to time throughout our discussion. It is about consciousness. Are Cedric and Super-Cedric, and even Charlie and Harry Smith, conscious or not?

The answer is at one level embodied in the philosophical chestnut of so-called 'Other Minds', and we shall try to cook the chestnut later. But in the meantime, as a preliminary, I shall suggest two things. Cedric is, as I have shown, 'aware of' the edges of lines. But awareness may be a matter of degree, increasing – as in the case of the development of the multiplicity of the necessary nerve fibres in the brain – until it reaches a state which will allow the formation of images. 'I remember Charlie' and I have a faded sensory effect (a faded photograph) which I call an image, and then I use language and words like 'I' and 'aware', and these are all terms referring to events inside myself or to myself *in toto*. It is here that we see the advent of consciousness rendered mature by language, as is perhaps inevitable with complexity.

So while Cedric may not be conscious – or is only partially so – Super-Cedric, certainly when he becomes vocal, we are going to assert is *bound to be* conscious, because it will be argued (and this will be a feature of later discussions) that no system of the complexity of man could succeed as he has succeeded and not be conscious. Consciousness is a property of the type of complexity which constitutes highly intelligent systems. As soon as a system includes itself in plans and refers to itself in complex verbal images, it can no longer be said to be non-conscious: this is a basic supposition.

3 Machine Thinking

He did what he was born to do,
Proved some assumptions were untrue.

W. H. Auden, *New Year Letter*

A man-machine is made in man's image largely because man makes it, and he is copying – or trying to copy – himself. When we are dealing with a problem, in trying to reproduce humanlike behaviour artificially, we ask ourselves how we personally would deal with it and we try to build the answer into Cedric and Super-Cedric.

Copying our own thinking is more difficult than copying our own arm movements, because we cannot so easily see ourselves think. One thing, though, should console us and that is that we do think, and so what has been done once can be done again, by copying the process, at least in the first instance.

This process of copying is a natural method of approaching the problem of reproducing our own cognitive processes and it is used as a guideline to the accuracy of our machine blueprint of man, as well as the actual implementation of that blueprint. The result will not always be a copy of man's mechanism, precisely because we are not always aware of how our own mechanism actually works and therefore cannot copy it, or at least cannot be sure of copying it accurately. If we solve a problem we may be roughly aware of how we did so; we gathered all the relevant information, or as much of it as we could, and then formulated hypotheses about how the trick had to be – or had been – done. It is very much like a detective solving a murder case. The main principle involved throughout (at this stage) is to achieve the same end-results as man, but not necessarily by using the same means, and certainly not by using the same fabric.

What this means is that we need to have some idea of how information is gathered together, and of the way in which it is utilized to model ourselves. We make a comparison between the way the behaviour occurs in both man and the machine copy.

It can then be seen how it can all be placed into an appropriate causal description. This sort of description simply makes clear what caused what in a whole string of events (Jack kicks over the kettle and the kettle scalds the dog and the dog is taken to the vet . . .) There is no sense, though, in which any of this by itself explains what part of the human brain is operating.

There are other means of putting the pieces of the jigsaw together, and these will be tried if and when they are needed. It is indeed very much like reconstructing a picture, a symbolic picture in the main, of events that have already occurred. It is a difficult and complicated process which lays emphasis on one very important point: the distinction we must make between synthesis and simulation.

By *simulation* we mean copying: the methods by which we copy the brainlike processes at the behavioural (including introspective) level and the neurophysiological level, the level of brain activity. It is impossible, as yet, to check whether or not the copying is accurate in detail and we must necessarily leave gaps of some uncertainty in our blueprint. This uncertainty is accepted, and need in no way be a barrier to the main goal of building Super-Cedric.

These gaps, though, do not in any case occur in any synthesis. By a *synthesis* we mean the building of a system which works, regardless of the methods used. A simulation purports to use the same methods and achieve the same ends as the system copied, while a synthesis achieves the same ends and is not concerned with whether or not the methods employed are the same.

We are saying that Jack's behaviour can be copied (simulated) by programming a computer to behave just as he behaves. But the same goals of intelligent activity would be achieved by totally different synthetic means. In neither case is it necessary to make Jack just as he is.

There is another step involved and this is the *fabric* in which the manufacturing is done. Even in our simulation we are not yet concerned with using the same fabric; the building materials are metallic and electronic and not as yet colloidal protoplasmic, and although the latter undoubtedly will be used in the future, as a material it is quite unnecessary to the main cause of making machines think.

It may well be that a metallic fabric would make for a more efficient species than the human one. Such a species would probably also use wheels rather than legs, because they are more efficient. If so, of course, it would certainly influence architects to build differently: we would have buildings (like multi-storey car parks) with slopes rather than stairs, and all the other appropriate environmental features, features which are appropriate to the 'metallic' rather than the 'protoplasmic' form.

Another point which is worth pondering over now is the relationship between the copying process and the synthetic process. When we synthesize, we cannot ignore the model of ourselves and other human beings, and it is arguable that we cannot synthesize other than by trying to simulate. But this, on closer inspection, is probably not true, because there are a number of different ways in which the visual sense, for example, can be simulated, and presumably they cannot *all* be on the same pattern as in the human eye and the visual system. We can allow for the possibility that a complex mechanism like the visual system can be 'seen' in more than one way, and indeed could have more than one mode of operation built into it. But this must surely be fairly improbable. Certainly there must be a limit to the variety of the methods by which the eye functions. We shall, however, during our building operations, be aware that, at least in a general way, there must be only one criterion of success: the system must sense and perceive information, it must be able to store it and recall it when required, and it must be able to utilize it as and when it is needed.

Some thought must be given to putting flesh on the skeleton and also to asking if there is something about a 'biological' species that is essentially and inevitably different from a 'physical' (metallic as opposed to colloidal) species. At this point there seems no reason to think so, but further reflection on the matter will be necessary later. As an interim judgment one would guess that the growth period of protoplasmic systems changes their mode of acquiring information, though not the information acquired.

I pursue now the goal of a blueprint of man's behaviour and by doing so I build a number of different 'living' systems. I could (and once did) argue that the need for building the system and not merely preparing a blueprint stems from the need to show that our theories are effective, and by 'effective' I mean 'real' blueprints, i.e. what the blueprint says can really be translated into a sensing-processing-acting system.

Before starting to discuss the details in terms of artefacts like Cedric and man-machines like Super-Cedric, it is as well to remember that the ideas being developed are by no means original. What is original is the ability to implement them.

Tribute should be paid to Democritus and other early Greek philosophers who were in some important ways distinct from the Platonists. Democritus thought in more materialist and 'scientific' terms than Plato, and pursued a line of thought which was wholly in the spirit of modern cybernetics.

Cybernetics means, of course, the science of control and communication in animals, men and machines – or at least this was Norbert Wiener's definition, and he was the founder of cybernetics.

Cybernetics is actually the science of 'artificial intelligence', which is what this book is concerned with, and, although as far as I know, Democritus and the other Greek thinkers of his ilk never actually said 'men are machines' in any sense of that admittedly ambiguous phrase, they were certainly thinking along those lines. Later, the eighteenth-century Mechanistic Materialists quite explicitly said 'men are machines', a sentiment which has since been echoed by many. What none of them was able to do was produce the evidence needed to prove their point, by actually going ahead and starting to build a man-machine.

As a first approximation I shall repeat what I said at the beginning of this book, that by the phrase 'man is a machine' we mean that it is in principle possible (and will one day in practice be possible) to construct a human being by artificial means in the laboratory. If someone then says, 'But that would not, *by definition*, be a human being', we could counter by saying that we mean 'something which would be indistinguishable from a human being, at first in its behaviour and later in *all* essential respects'.

The phrase 'construct by artificial means' means 'other than by the normal sexual means' and other than by such methods as artificial insemination. It would be quite acceptable to achieve our end by manufacturing a seed or an embryo which grew like a human in an environment, but at this time we are thinking of producing the readymade adult system.

I should mention again the problem of 'Other Minds'. This is based on the simple idea that we cannot be sure of anyone else's consciousness, or that others have awareness in the same way as we do. This reservation, of course, applies to people, to machines or to anything else. It is this consideration which leads us to say that we decide a person is conscious (and that certainly includes all *normal* people) if they behave more or less as we do. This has the consequence that a machine will be thought of as humanlike if it *behaves* as human beings do.

Next we have to add that appearance is not relevant to our first cause, only intelligence and ability are, and this leads us to the Turing Interrogation Game.

The original game is one in which we have discourse with two people, one a man and the other a woman, and we have to guess which is which. Since their voices are irrelevant (presumably) to their intelligence, we carry out the discourse in writing, and since even the writing may provide an irrelevant clue, we should have it typed. Each can say 'I am a man' or 'I am a woman' and so on, but this could be a bluff and the only way we can make the distinction is by the nature of our questions and their answers.

We are being asked to decide what characteristics (apart from body-structure, voice, etc) distinguish a man from a woman. This turns out to be very difficult. It simply underlines the point that if two systems behave in the same way, we have to assume that they *are* the same. A system can be any collection of elements which make it a cohesive whole. A system is sometimes called a 'black box' if you cannot open it. The Turing Game asks whether two black boxes which you cannot see are distinguishable or not.

If we now substitute a 'machine' for one of the human beings and ask if we can make the necessary distinction in the Interrogation Game, we have the problem of deciding once more in terms of what seem to be the essentials. If we cannot tell, then we have done the trick. In other words, if one cannot distinguish a man from a machine in this situation, then in the important sense we are concerned with, they are the same.

This is not, of course, a definition of a machine or of an artificially intelligent system, but it is a good indicator or test of the existence of such a system. In fact, the test can be passed already, since certain artificially constructed dialogues do the trick, but there is at the moment a certain sleight of hand involved – it is really the programmer at work still; soon, there will be no sleight of hand at all.

This development started in recent times on the east coast of America at the beginning of World War II, when a number of scientists and philosophers got together to study problems in the science of information processing and in particular in the study of automatic control systems for locating and firing at enemy aircraft. The old manual methods were no longer any use because of the high speeds of modern aircraft. The resulting control systems were then seen as being very similar in operation to the human brain and with the simultaneous development of high-speed digital computers, it became clear how human intelligence might in some circumstances be *synthesized*.

The men involved in this early movement included the same John von Neumann who was later concerned with machine reproduction; Norbert Wiener, the founder member of the group; Warren McCulloch, brain expert; F. C. S. Northrop, philosopher; Julian Bigelow, information scientist; and Arturio Rosenbleuth, neurologist. There were other interested parties, but these constituted the central group. The result was the new great push to construct machines which think, leading to the present advanced state of affairs.

Since the first burst of enthusiasm, a great deal has taken place. This is so even though the original protagonists began armed only with the belief that a major effort would supply the blueprint the biologists and medical scientists were looking for, leaving out of consideration the enormous dangers involved. It was only subsequently (and increasingly) that we have come to see the huge moral problem posed. It is also a political, social and, in general, a very practical problem, for some people essentially more practical than moral. But I shall return to the central processing involved in our machine models, Cedric and Super-Cedric.

So far we have been primarily concerned with perception. We have seen that the senses involved can be very primitive, as in Cedric, or very complex, as in Super-Cedric, and they can range from simple sensors to complicated cameras and radios or their equivalent, and to the need for classification systems that make up and record every combination of what is sensed. All this information is then transmitted to the central processor, which, at least in the first instance, is concerned with the visual processing. It then moves onwards to the 'more central', more detailed, comparisons with stored memories.

The different senses are registered and classified independently and are almost certainly sent to the temporary memory store (sometimes called Short-Term Memory, or STM for short) where they are classified, together with information from the other senses. The snapshots are compared with the sounds and the smells and tastes, if they exist, as well as with the pictures already in the snapshot album.

The reasons for this separate form of classification in the human brain are doubtless bound up with the 'accidental' biological facts of evolution. But it also serves a useful purpose in what some people have been pleased to call 'neuroeconomy'. By classifying the senses and their information input separately at first, and then proceeding in stages, the brain needs many less nerve cells than if all the senses were classified together in one fell swoop. The second stage of operations is classification with regard to all the senses and the lodging of information in the Long-Term Memory (LTM).

There are short cuts in the human brain which, by taking an alternative path through the lower parts of the forebrain (the thalamus and hypothalamus) enable the person to be alerted to a state of emergency. This is obviously bound up with emotional and emergency behaviour which I shall describe in more detail later.

Suffice it to say that, for rational behaviour, the system works more elaborately and in stages, with considerable redundancy, and is involved in the questions of 'What is it?' or 'What are they?' and, in general, 'What is going on?' and then, more centrally, 'What do I do about it?'

Cedric, in general, has to recognize only a few features of the environment. It has to distinguish between going left, going right, stopping, turning around and going back, and going straight on. It also has to distinguish between a state of being 'hungry' or 'thirsty', of 'searching' and of 'lying dormant'.

Cedric's sensors record a line, and when the line turns right the sensors track to the right and activate the right turning of the wheels on which it runs in order to follow the line. The fact is recorded in its store as an ordered count (think of a person in a maze simply saying to himself, 'Maze A, first turn right', and writing it down).

It then proceeds to the next choice-point (or point of change) and repeats the operation; this time, if a choice is involved, 'Go straight on, but could have turned left'. Eventually, the maze being completed by the discovery of food and assuming that Cedric was in a state of hunger, the series of events is complete, as is its record.

Now maze A may be only one of a number of mazes. Think of mazes A, B, C, D, E, F, and so on. Let each maze be different and provide a number of choice-points. The following could be a typical maze, say A:

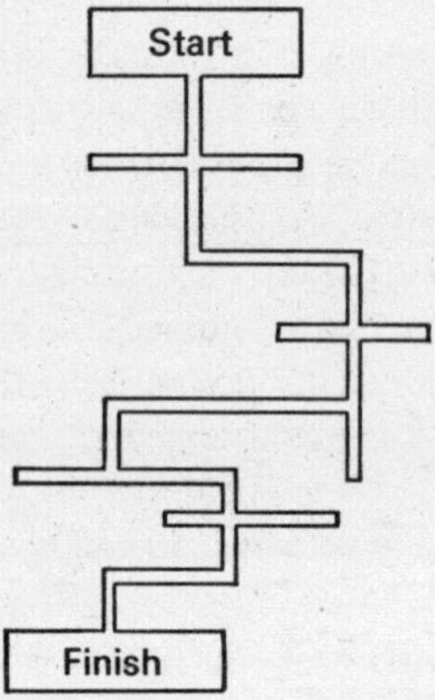

This is correctly run in the following way: each choice-point requires a decision and there will be other nodal points where choices need not be made but turns must be.

The correct solution is: Start-S(straight on)-L(turn left)-R(turn right)-S-R-L-L-R-S-R-L-Finish.

The sequence is made up of: Start-C(choice)-NC(no choice)-NC-C-NC-NC-C-NC-C-NC-NC-Finish. The assumption here is that NC (no choice) means that you simply turn left, or whatever. It is true that you could always turn back, but you could do this at any time and therefore this will not be thought of as a 'choice' as such. A turning-back would be appropriate only at a dead end. In maze B, which is as follows, it could be appropriate at the third choice-point and indeed at any of the 'more obvious' blind alleys:

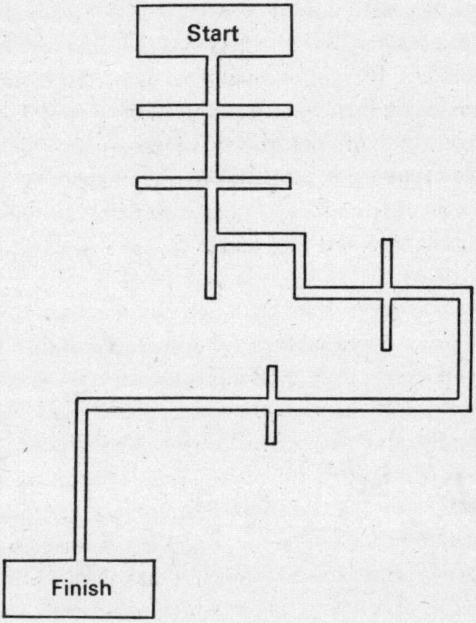

The correct solution here is: Start-S-S-L-R-L-S-R-R-S-L-Finish.

Now consider just these two mazes A and B and the behaviour of the artefact in them.

It travels up maze A and may turn left or right, but eventually – if not the first time – it goes straight on, then left, then right and straight on again at the next choice-point. This is recorded, and when the maze is finished a correct route is noted: as a result, turns made unsuccessfully are eliminated. This requires 'realizing' that to take a blind alley is a mistake, and this is a sort of higher-level form of knowledge. This allows Cedric to dispense with information about blind alleys (it may of course keep such information if it is required for other purposes, as it may be) and then, when it is placed in A, to run straight from start to finish without a mistake. We note in passing that even for such a very simple task Cedric needs more information *while learning* than he needs after he *has learned*.

The other point we should notice is that a mistake is noted, but is not repeated, whereas a success is noted and is repeated (remember OAX and how it was learned). The principle involved is the so-called Law of Effect: we repeat successes and do not repeat failures. If emotions had been involved, as they will be later on, then we would have an example of the Freudian pleasure-pain principle which implies that we repeat success/pleasure and do not repeat (but even actively avoid) failure/pain. As far as Cedric is concerned, this means that the simple storage register 'plugs in' a correct turn and does not plug in the incorrect one.

We now come to an important step for Cedric. It must recognize that maze A and maze B are different, and this it does by first running B as if it were A (assuming it learns A first) and this leads to a mistake at the second choice-point. Then it gradually runs B correctly, and a comparison with A shows that they are different, and it can then run them both. If there is no other distinguishing factor (colour, smell, etc) and if it has the requisite sensors, it will detect a 'choice' as opposed to a forced turn at the second step of the maze. This means that it can not only recognize but can also discriminate, which means recognizing the difference between more than one input-stimulus.

Given these basic attributes it can now (given also sufficient storage space) easily collect 'maps' of all the mazes it meets, and we should remember that it makes no difference in principle whether it is one maze changing from time to time or different fixed and unchanging mazes: the learning process remains the same. Clearly the discrimination needed to recognize the maze might be different according to where the differences lie, and this is especially true of the first difference. Therefore, if C had a right turn and D a left turn at the first choice-point where both gave both alternatives, then Cedric would have to run down one way and hope it was correct. Any rule can be programmed in for this, but the easiest thing perhaps is for Cedric to do the same as it did on the last occasion. This weights its memory for recency and is a better way of memorizing records if the mazes are changing, and it is also convenient as a rule which has also to be remembered: it implies that the time of the runs is kept or, and this is the equivalent, the record of the runs is kept in successive registers. This can be done in any number of ways.

The whole problem of maze-running can now be made more difficult by introducing mazes with alternative successful routes. Cedric can still find the best route by keeping a record of each route and taking the one with the least turns. The rule it must now follow is always to take the route with the minimum number of turns. The basis of such a rule is that when it recognizes a thirsty state it seeks water and seeks it at maximum convenience (i.e. with the minimum of delay).

Cedric can show what is sometimes called 'latent learning'. It learns where the turnings are that it does *not* take in running maze A, so that if maze A were changed but had the first three nodal points the same, it would remember where else to try, because it already knows the alternative it previously rejected.

Our artefact is now becoming quite sophisticated in its behaviour and we shall build further on these simple beginnings. But we should note two things. One is that very large numbers of problems met by adult human beings are surprisingly like maze-running problems, because they are sequential, and demand the learning of the correct responses at choice-points and the following of simple rules. The second point is that the learning of new tricks requires more 'brain' (in the form of computer 'chips') being loaded on to Cedric and soon its power/weight ratio will let it down, so that it simply will not be able to carry its brain about with it.

The main intellectual step still required by Cedric (or by Super-Cedric) is to start to generalize systematically on its capacity for maze-running, so that it can think of turning left or right in a maze as choosing red or blue at a choice-point, or doing any one thing rather than another. This is a little reminiscent of Boolean algebra, and so, with a word of reassurance to those who hate algebra and do not know of George Boole, I shall explain why he and his work are relevant.

Boolean algebra is concerned with what George Boole originally called the laws of human thought. He called them this because the mathematics he devised seemed to him to accurately mirror the processes of human thought.

These ideas did not establish themselves very quickly when he first proposed them over a hundred years ago. His work eventually became widely recognized but by then his algebra was regarded as being only indirectly connected with the way the human brain works. Let us just look at these ideas.

Consider a number of classes of objects or events. Call them A, B, C... By a class we can mean 'all red objects', 'all tall objects' or, of course, 'all quick events', 'all slow events'. Indeed, a class is any collection of items, objects or events you care to think about, which we arrive at by parcelling up the world around us in the manner we do. Regardless of how we interpret our classes, we just call them A, B, C... and then we use certain operators (sometimes called connectives) on them so that we get A′, B′, C′ ... which is not-A, not-B, not-C. If A is all red objects, then A′ is all the other objects in the world, i.e. all not-red objects.

Next we can conjoin two classes A and B, which we write $A \cap B$, so that the conjoint class is all the objects that are both A *and* B. Similarly we can disjoin two classes A and B, so that we get A *or* B or both. This is written $A \cup B$. This is the inclusive sense of the word 'or' as opposed to the exclusive sense normal in English. We normally say we will go to the cinema or the theatre, but we mean the choice to be exclusive and we do not mean to imply that we are going to both.

So we now have the beginnings of a formal logical system of algebra which can be represented by an axiomatic system. I shall not discuss Boolean algebra in great detail but merely outline it informally.

Another basic notion of Boolean algebra, with which we might have started, is that of class membership. We say $a \in A$ and by this we mean 'the individual element, or member, belongs to (symbolized by the Greek letter epsilon, or $\in$) the class A'. Similarly, $a \notin A$ means 'a is *not* a member of A'. We also have a relationship between classes, symbolized $A \subset B$, which is meant to characterize 'class inclusion'. This means that all members of class A are included in class B. The relationship can be represented as follows:

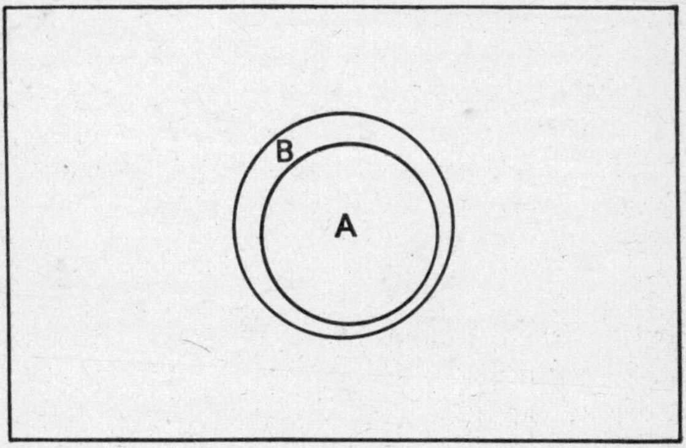

We need to be able to distinguish between class inclusion and class membership. 'Fred' is an individual and is a member of the class of 'human beings'. 'Freds' are the class of all people of the name 'Frederick' who are included in the class 'human being'. The whole question is made slightly arbitrary by the fact that classes can of course be *nul* (have no members) or have one member (a unit class), whereas an individual is to be thought of as one member of a larger group. A unit class and an individual can, however, if necessary, be intentionally confounded.

The type of diagram shown above is sometimes called an Euler-Venn diagram and can be conveniently used to represent class relationships. The rectangle represents the entire universe and A and B, whether overlapping or not, are any two classes in the universe.

We can now conjoin two classes A and B, as I have said, and we write this $A \cap B$; by it we mean those members of the classes A and B which are common to both. For example, this time A is 'all green objects' and B is 'all square objects'; then $A \cap B$ (read as 'A *cap* B' or 'A *and* B') is the conjunction class of 'all green (and) square objects'. The Euler-Venn diagram is as follows, and shows $A \cap B$ as a shaded area:

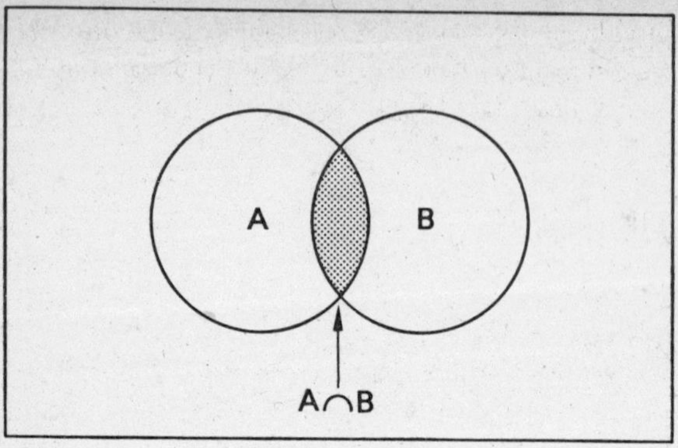

Similarly A ∪ B (read as 'A *cup* B' or 'A *or* B') is used to define the disjunction of the classes A and B, where if A is 'all green objects' and B is 'all square objects', then A ∪ B is made up of 'all green objects or square objects or both, and all green objects of all shapes and all square objects of any colour'. The Euler-Venn diagram is as follows, and shows A ∪ B shaded:

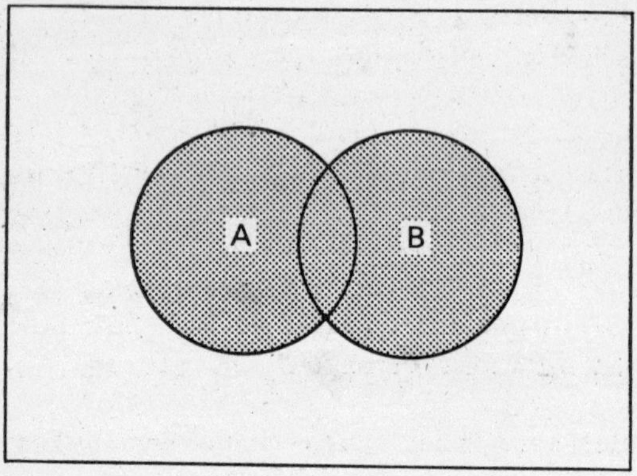

It will be clear that in our discussion of Boolean algebra we are using capital letters A, B . . ., N to represent classes, and lower-case letters a, b . . ., n to represent individuals.

Another basic relationship in Boolean algebra, the one we

started with, is that of negation (or complementation). We write A′ for not-A and represent it in an Euler-Venn diagram as:

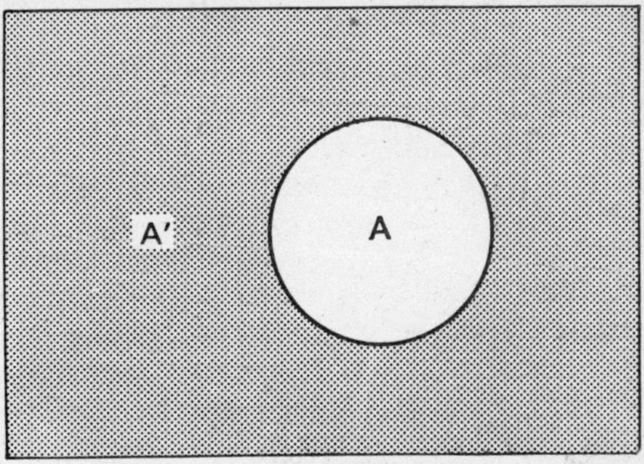

A′ is the shaded area, and we say that if A is 'all red objects' then A′ is 'all objects which are not red'. Because A′ refers to only one class, we call this (negation) a singular or monadic relation, while relations between two classes such as $A \cap B$ and $A \cup B$ are binary or dyadic relations.

Two special cases, one of which I have already mentioned, are the nul class, which contains nothing and is symbolized by 0, and the universal class which contains everything and is symbolized by 1 (or sometimes I); the 1 is represented by the rectangle of the Euler-Venn diagram.

We can apply the operation of negation to each of these, and naturally enough we get the negation or 'opposite' class, so:

$$0' = 1$$
$$1' = 0$$

and we can also say for any class A that $A \cap A' = 0$, $A \cup A' = 1$

since clearly a class has no overlap with its negation, and equally clearly a class and its negation make up everything. It is also clear that we are assuming here that classes are *definite* (precisely defined) and we can always decide whether any individual is, or is not, a member of the class.

There are a large number of operations among Boolean classes that are very similar to those of arithmetic. Thus we can say that if $A = B$, then $B = A$, where all members of A are also members of B, and vice versa. Similarly, if $A = B$ and $B = C$, then $A = C$, and again we have such relations as:

$$A \cap B = B \cap A \tag{1}$$

$$A \cup B = B \cup A \tag{2}$$

$$A \cap (B \cap C) = (A \cap B) \cap C \tag{3}$$

$$A \cup (B \cup C) = (A \cup B) \cup C \tag{4}$$

$$A \cap A = A \cup A = A \tag{5}$$

$$A \cap (B \cup C) = (A \cap B) \cup (A \cap C) \tag{6}$$

$$A \cup (B \cap C) = (A \cup B) \cap (A \cup C) \tag{7}$$

$$A \cup 0 = A \cap 1 = A \tag{8}$$

$$(A')' = A \tag{9}$$

and so on, where there is a close analogy between conjunction and disjunction and multiplication and addition. All the ordinary laws of arithmetic apply in the same way to Boolean algebra.

Let us look at the Euler-Venn diagrams for the relations

$$A \cap (B \cap C) = (A \cap B) \cap C \tag{10}$$

and

$$A \cup (B \cup C) = (A \cup B) \cup C \tag{11}$$

The first is:

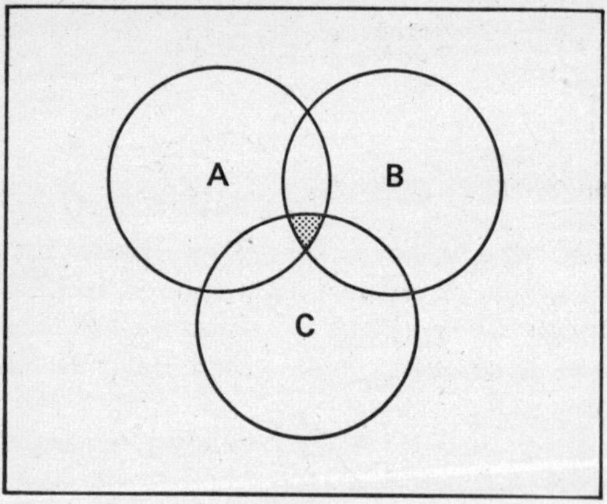

and applies to both the left-hand side and the right-hand side of (10). The same applies to the Euler-Venn diagram for (11), which is:

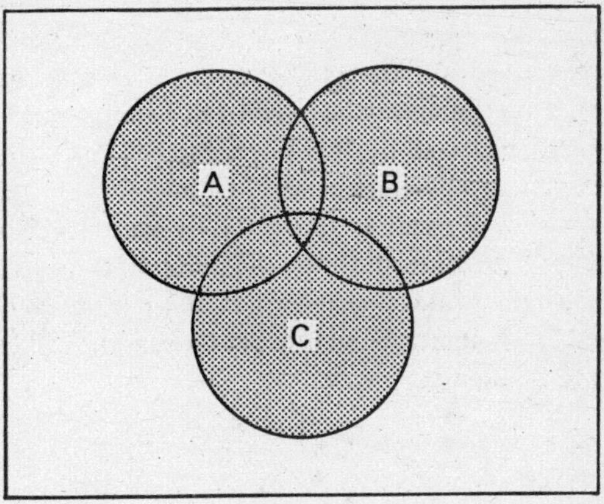

We can also write our classes A, B . . ., N in terms of their individual members a, b . . ., n, so that if $A = \{a, b, c, d\}$ and $B = \{a, b, d, e\}$ then $A \cap B = \{a, b, d\}$; which simply makes clear that a, b and d occur in both A and B, i.e. in $A \cap B$. Similarly, if $C = \{a, c, e, f, g\}$ then

$$A \cap (B \cap C) = \{a\}$$

since a is the only member common to A, B and C. It follows, of course, from what has already been said, that

$$(A \cap B) \cap C = \{a\}$$

since

$$(A \cap B) \cap C = A \cap (B \cap C)$$

also

$$A \cup B = \{a, b, c, d, e\}$$

and therefore

$$A \cup (B \cup C) = \{a, b, c, d, e, f, g\}$$

and also

$$A \cap (B \cup C) = \{a, b, c, d\}.$$

I shall leave the symbolism at this point. But we must, however, draw some important conclusions.

Cedric is a Boolean system, since all the workings of computers from the largest available digital computer right down to the smallest – like Cedric – have chip boards which are Boolean in function. George Boole was not far wrong in believing that his logic depicted human thought, and the reason is that in all situations a description *can* be reduced to a simple binary choice which is to-do or not-to-do, 'to be or not to be', in the end.

These Boolean operators of AND, OR and NOT can be reproduced in hardware terms as AND-gates, OR-gates and NOT-gates. The following diagrams illustrate the point where we say that 2 is the 'threshold' of the element which will not fire its output C unless both of its inputs A and B fire at the same time. Here is the AND-gate in Figure 1:

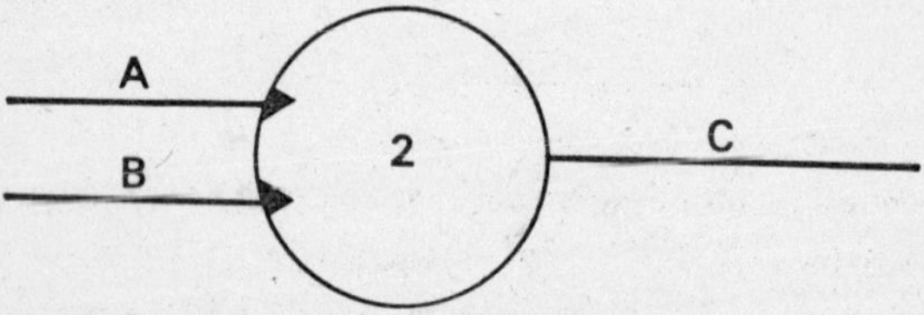

Figure 1

We say, in Boolean algebra, that C fires at time t if and only if A and B both fire at time t—1 (the instant before) in symbols that can be written:

$$C_t \equiv A_{t-1} \cap B_{t-1}$$

where ≡ means 'if and only if'.

Figure 2 shows the OR-gate, where only the threshold number has changed from 2 to 1, so now A *or* B alone can fire C:

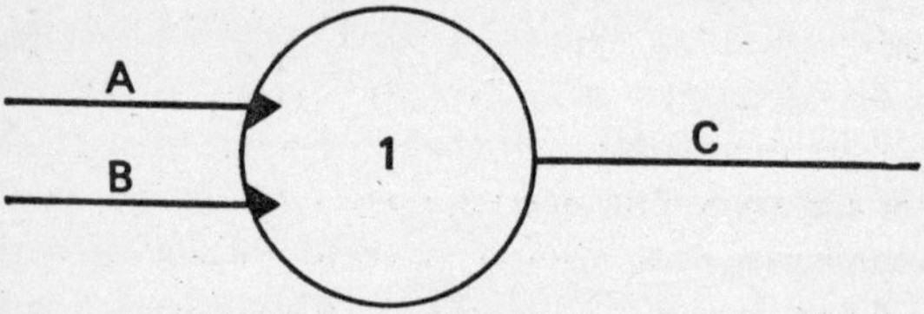

Figure 2

C fires at time t if and only if A or B (or both) fire at time t—1.

$$C_t \equiv A_{t-1} \cup B_{t-1}$$

Finally, the NOT-gate which requires the inhibitor ending which stops firing rather than starts it. If we now use the threshold O, we mean to imply that the element fires unless it is actively stopped, or in other words it spontaneously fires unless inhibited.

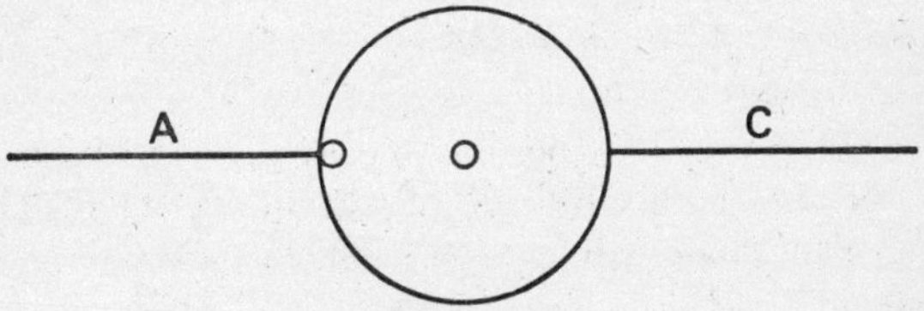

Figure 3

C does not fire at t if and only if A fires at t—1.

$$C'_t \equiv A_{t-1}$$

It is not difficult to guess that these gates are easy to reproduce in hardware, and indeed the chips and logic boards of micro-processors which are popular in modern computers, and are also used by Cedric, are full of just such gates.

I shall be returning again later to this topic and the other questions raised by logic. But it might be guessed at this point that when it was thought that Boole was wrong, and that human beings were never as precise or idealized as operating in a form like Boolean algebra, his critics were wrong in thinking that the human nervous system *could not* work this way – because it could and it does. At one time, of course, people were not even sure that thinking was carried out by the brain.

One of the main discoveries (perhaps 'realizations' would be a better word) made by Norbert Wiener and his associates was that the nervous system was a Boolean type of switching system. Before a well-meaning neurophysiologist or brain specialist jumps in and says, 'But a description of the nervous system is more complicated than Boolean algebra', our answer is that it may be *at some level* of description but not at the level of a control system.

If we describe the nervous system at the electrical and chemical level then of course our Boolean description is not appropriate and our description can be in the form of differential equations, chemical formulae or whatever is appropriate. This in no way precludes a description of the nervous system, couched entirely in terms of a set of simple either-or switches which could quite easily be described in Boolean algebra. It is an interesting thought that the whole of the human brain could be described by one gigantic Boolean formula.

We should note also in passing that Boolean algebra is an axiomatic system like Euclidean geometry. This writing-up of a system into axioms (or postulates) and theorems and rules of inference is much like describing a machine in blueprint form. Methods of proof within such axiomatic systems are either *algorithmic* (exhaustive and precise) or *heuristic* (short cuts and uncertain) and these methods prove to be very important to our search for intelligent machines, since much of the haphazard type of information-processing and the making of off-the-cuff plans and decisions is essentially heuristic in nature.

So Cedric can learn and Super-Cedric, which is just Cedric with a huge brain, can learn even more obviously. This means that they are adaptive and can change as circumstances change. They do not do only what they were programmed to do (remember Lady Lovelace) any more than humans do. Both man and machines are adaptive and capable of self-organization (self-programming). They are essentially also goal-seeking, since no behaviour, certainly no intelligent adaptive behaviour, is possible unless it is purposive and unless after the behaviour is complete, reinforcement takes place.

It is necessary now to show the higher ramifications of Cedric's logic chips and boards as it groans under its growing superstructure. So much does it groan that, as has been frequently warned, it becomes remotely controlled by its brain which is left at home.

In human terms we simply mean that a person attempts to do something by some method because he is motivated to do so, and after he has finished he must know the result. He can never learn, never improve, unless he has 'knowledge of results'. Imagine getting better at darts if you never see where your darts land with respect to the dart-board. So it is that our 'learning machine' must have the characteristic of control by the 'feedback' of information.

Now to the so-called higher cognitive activities – especially thinking, and rational thinking at that. The use of the word 'rational' suggests logic, and the spectre of George Boole looms up again, as well as that of feedback of results of actions.

I propose to state that Super-Cedric, which we may think of as the mask of an intelligent person (rather like a ventriloquist's dummy) beyond which is the usual large computer room *without* the usual human control panel, can pick up information and learn the structure of mazes. We are then reminded that much human thinking is like maze-running: even complicated intelligent games like chess are a sort of elaborate run down a maze, and certainly noughts-and-crosses (OAX) is just that. So perhaps, as has been hinted, full-scale human intelligence can be manufactured by building upon these same building bricks, and by simply using many more of them.

Thinking is partly a matter of ruminating over events remembered, where the human memory supplies faded pictures (they are called images), and learning, and, perhaps above all, learning and problem-solving through the use of a symbolic model of the world. This is where language comes in. In the next chapter I shall look at language and how it can be learned by machines in just the same way as human beings learned.

Thinking is a process of systematic association and it applies to both images (browsing over our snapshot album) and symbols (considering systematic descriptions of the evidence, in a murder case, for example). All this goes on in the human brain, and, as far as is known, in exactly the same way in the computer, precisely because we make it so.

4 Language

If he contends . . . that he has defined all his terms and proved all his propositions, then either he is a performer of logical miracles or he is an ass, and, as you know, logical miracles are impossible.

Cassius J. Keyser

We have considered some aspects of the sensing and central processing of both Cedric and Super-Cedric. This especially involves the *classification* and storage of information and the *association* of information such that an identified event or set of events is associated with a satisfactory response.

Basically, the stimulus-response (input-output) connections are built into the system. They are represented in organisms by instinctive behaviour patterns, and in Cedric by pre-wired connections. In Super-Cedric they are also pre-wired, but are clearly capable of being made conditional, or more sophisticated, should our copying processes seem to demand it.

The result of superimposing highly conditional connections on the pre-wired ones is the same as superimposing learning, thinking and the other cognitive faculties upon the simple (or relatively simple) instinctive ones. To some extent, the potential for conditional learning is contingent upon the size and structure of the system and it is also contingent upon the experience encountered in the environment.

The conditional (or contingent) nature of events and their recording is of great importance, and closely bound up with learning. Whenever we are confronted by a choice – take, for instance, the simplest sort of Boolean 'yes-no' choice situation – we are acting, in the actual choosing, in a conditional manner. On what basis is a choice made? In Cedric as a maze-runner it was either random (initially) or on the basis of 'remembering' that left meant food and right meant no-food.

In a hardware model, a switch in the on-state could provide one result in meeting a new situation and in the off-state it could provide a different result. A switch 'on' could mean light or heat, and a switch 'off' could mean dark or cold. Ordinary light switches are just like this.

Computer programs also have these conditional links whereby a new order is taken from location X if 'a is greater than b' and from Y if 'a is not greater than b'. So if a = b = 2, then the next order is taken from Y. It is rather like a train that switches tracks according to the state of the points: these take it left in some circumstances and right in others.

In this regard should be mentioned a type of change and development called maturation. This is made up of a series of nervous connections which are brought about by age, and the behaviour observed in the grown animal (including the human being) is contingent both upon the connections and the environment.

The classical example of maturation is the swimming activity of the salamander. The first reflex movements of the salamander occur when certain neural connections are made and the whole set of reflexes occur only when *all* the neural connections are made. The environment must include the water, without which the salamander's ultimate ability to swim would make no sense.

It goes without saying that we can, in Super-Cedric, build-in these activities which depend upon the completion of certain circuits, but it is by no means obvious that such delay in growth serves any useful purpose. It should be regarded rather as yet another biological accident which occurs simply because real organisms grow from seeds; it should therefore be noted, but not included, in the machine design.

We now meet the most important aspect of human behaviour. It is an aspect which is quite crucial to the success of the whole operation. It is language.

It is clear that language (communication) becomes important to Cedric in a social context when a second artefact (call him Cedric 2) is introduced, so that they can relate to each other their experience, and, given a much bigger world in which to operate, they can share the efforts of discovering all about it. To make this sharing effective they have to be able to describe their experience to one another. If we (or they) labelled the logic chips and logic boards with what they meant (input a is the start to maze A, b is the first choice in maze B and so on) then we need only show them to one another. But to avoid the necessity of being opened up, Cedric simply writes (or says) what its labels are.

This presupposes that languages are available for Cedric 1 to talk to Cedric 2 and vice versa. For this to be so, such a language has to satisfy the usual conditions, i.e. the words (symbols) used must refer to the same thing for both Cedric 1 and Cedric 2 and the words should be combined in a meaningful way. The rules of meaning are notoriously difficult to state, but are not so difficult to use, since even tiny children who can hardly speak often communicate quite effectively with one another.

In a sense the addition of an artificial voice to our two (now Super-) Cedrics is irrelevant to what is important in their language. It is a fact, however, that speech synthesizers and speech recognition systems are in the process of development.

You will have to take it on trust that the Cedrics in a tiny way, and the Super-Cedrics in a very large way, can use language, and it will be explained later how they do so. For the moment let us do what we usually do when copying: look at language, and at why it became essential in human beings.

It might be added that existing computer languages (and this includes a fair copy of everyday English) are regularly used, with as much syntactic precision as is necessary and certainly more than a human being normally uses.

One way of looking at the beginnings of language means that we must turn, briefly, to the psychologically based movement called behaviourism. This is a movement which emphasizes the 'machinelike' nature of human thinking and learning. It all started with Pavlov's famous dogs, and when he noticed that the sight of the person who normally fed them was enough to make them salivate, even without the presence of the meat they ate. This was because of the previous association that had been set up between the person and the meat, and the satisfaction derived from eating the meat when hungry. Pavlov called the meat the *unconditioned stimulus*, the person was the *conditioned stimulus* and the salivating was both the *conditioned* and the *unconditioned* response. It was soon realized that the conditioned and the unconditioned responses were not in fact the same; they differed in amount and also, to some extent, in kind. At the same time they were very similar; indeed, so similar that at first they were thought to be identical.

The unconditioned response is innate or 'built-in' to the animal from birth (pre-wired in Cedric) while the conditioned response is learned or conditioned, and involves elements of curiosity and surprise in some cases, as well as salivation.

All animals could be so conditioned. This means that Cedric learns that a bell, say, *means* (is associated with) food.

It is of interest here that 'means' is a reasonable interpretation of 'is associated with', much like denoting or labelling in ordinary language.

A second-order conditioned stimulus-response association could be set up by first setting up an ordinary conditioned association. So we say that food is associated with the sight of a person. If we now ring a bell before the person arrives, we can achieve a second-order association. We flash a light before the bell is rung, and provided these various stimuli were all associated for a sufficiently long time, the light alone would produce the conditioned response of salivation: there is a third-order conditioned stimulus-response association.

Many other experimental results followed which showed that conditioning could be thought of in terms of simply *reward training*, where, by begging, the dog is given food; or *escape training*, where a cat standing on an electrified floor can escape by running; and *avoidance training*, where the occurrence of a flash of light before the shock causes the cat to leave the electrified floor. A prior association needs to be set up, so the animal must be shocked at least once.

Avoidance training is rather more subtle than escape training and shows the first important connection between signs and a state of expectation. This can occur for Cedric, since it records in store that A is followed by B; then in future when A occurs, B will probably follow.

The fourth type of training procedure is *secondary reward training*, and the classic example is that of teaching apes to perform a simple skilled activity for poker chips as rewards. They will do this and, later, cash in the poker chips for food. This is a clear-cut example of a symbolic type of activity, reminiscent of the use of money in human society, and it is a reminder that a close associative process is necessary in order to make the symbol meaningful, for this process can occur even with apes and lesser animals. This suggests that learning to acquire food, to escape from pain, and to avoid it when there is a warning given, leads directly on to language, which is learned in the same way.

All experiments of this sort are closely connected with the behaviouristic movement, which seeks to build an objective science of behaviour and rejects introspection as a method of the scientific study of behaviour. It is a first cousin to cybernetics. It is not difficult to see a Cedric society learning in precisely this way.

In the mainstream of semantics (the study of meaning in language), via the classic work of Ogden and Richards in *The Meaning of Meaning*, the same influence of behaviouristic conditioning theory exists. Alfred Korzybski talked of 'infinite-valued conditioning', by which he meant to draw attention to the fact that associations can be indefinitely remote from their original point of conditioning, and that language arises precisely by this same ordinary conditioning procedure. Others have pursued a somewhat different path from that of Korzybski and placed emphasis on the formal nature of signs and symbols, and have tried to construct precise languages, sometimes of an artificial kind such as occur in formal logic or computer languages.

Artificial languages can be made up of any collections of symbols whatever, put together according to certain rules; and we might cite, as examples, musical notation, chemical formulae, mathematics and mathematical logic, and Morse code. To take a simple example: say that our alphabet is X, Y, Z and W, and the only other symbol to be used is /, then our formal or artificial language (it is not a proper language yet, since it cannot be used to say anything intelligible) is made up of collections of these symbols, e.g. XY/XYY/XXZW//XYX, and so on.

The rules of grammar or syntax by which these symbols are correctly combined are now needed, and the rules themselves must be no part of the artificial language. These rules are part of what is called a 'meta-language'. If we now want to discuss the rules of syntax and make them precise (we call this process 'formalizing') then we shall need a meta-meta-language for the purpose, and so the process goes on indefinitely. The rules of grammar are concerned with the classification of word-types in a sentence, which has to be subject–predicate in form.

The idea of a meta-language is a simple one, and springs from the vital need to distinguish a word from whatever it is the word represents or 'stands for'. Words such as 'hungry', 'thirsty', describe organic states of hunger and thirst. Once this sort of distinction between word and object is made, we have a language which describes both a 'public' physical world and the world of 'private' ideas. We also have another language which describes the first language, and so on. Super-Cedric certainly needs a meta-language when it wants to talk about its language as opposed to talking about its actions and external events. After all, one does want to talk sometimes about language and so language must be self-referential.

Apart from the question of setting up a hierarchy of languages (and meta-languages) we are concerned not only with meaningless collections of symbols, however carefully arranged, but with languages that actually mean something to the users (i.e. convey information). And to convey information precisely, we need to state in the meta-language more rules than grammatical ones, in fact we also need semantic rules. These, in the simplest case, are rules which say, for example, 'let X stand for (or designate) Fred', 'Y designates Bill' and 'Z and W designate Charles and David', and then let / designate 'is followed by' and we can interpret our statement now as a description of some sort of ordering process like a queue: Fred and Bill start, and they are followed by Fred once again and Bill twice more, and so on. We could even regard the number of /s used as giving a measure of the time, and we might want to eliminate XX or YYY so that Bill could only occur once at a time (in each sub-queue), and so on. This means that we can, in language, distinguish the symbolic arrangement (grammar) from the meaning (semantics). Boolean algebra does just this with its symbols, so $\cap$ was 'and' and $\cup$ was 'or', and so on. Indeed, it is quite clear that Boolean algebra, and ordinary algebra and arithmetic, are all languages, in that they can be used for communication purposes.

But it should be noted that what we have just been doing

represents an attempt to make language increasingly *precise*, for these methods could also supply a clear-cut foundation for mathematics or logic, which we regard as languages, or at least frameworks for a language, until such time as they are actually used to communicate such information as is found in mechanics and in physics, for example. Mathematics, for instance, can be thought of as starting from a formal point of view, and then being used for descriptive purposes. This is clearly different from what was being attempted above in connection with behaviourism, where the emphasis was on the use of signs and how the signs (made up into 'natural languages') influenced actual behaviour. It is because of this that we can talk about logic, independent of logic users, but in doing so, great care must be taken, especially where meaning is involved.

The fields under discussion are as follows. *Syntax* is the body of grammatical rules by which sets of signs or languages are formed into sentences. *Semantics* is the process of adding rules of meaning, which ensures that the symbols are given meaning by way of reference. Semantics is concerned with the thing–word or sense–word relationship; and *pragmatics* is concerned with the way people behave in the total situation of sign-giving and sign-receiving.

The field has been further divided into the world of symbols and signs which has been given the collective name *semiotic*, and divided yet again, into pure and descriptive semiotic, which means pure and applied syntax, pure and applied semantics and pure and applied pragmatics. The important point is that 'intelligent machines' can be made to deal in such coinage as well as we can. In other words, Cedrics and Super-Cedrics must be able to communicate through language but must also be able to analyse such a language in syntactic, semantic and pragmatic terms.

We shall now look a little more carefully at the distinction between pure and descriptive semiotic. This distinction clearly applies to syntax and semantics, in being an account on one hand of the historical development of actual grammars and meanings; and at the other level of logic, it applies to the rules of artificial languages themselves and the analysis of languages from a formal point of view, concerned especially with meaning as opposed to an interest in the historical background of the languages. The distinction between pure and descriptive semiotic, at the level of pragmatics, has been challenged, as it is not easy to see how one can think of a 'formal situation' where people actually talk to each other. It seems to many researchers that words and their behavioural context are precisely (and can only be) a relationship of a factual kind. Many people feel that this same argument that 'pure' and 'descriptive' modes cannot really be distinguished applies to syntax and semantics and that the only way of sensibly discussing these matters is in the descriptive vein. However, this argument depends on the extent to which we can talk of the 'logical form' of arguments, as distinct from factual content in an actual linguistic situation. It does in fact seem reasonable to talk of 'pure pragmatics' since this can be understood as the formalization of descriptive pragmatics. This is simply the process of separating the symbols (and analysing them as such) from their use as signs.

By the term 'logical form', which we have already used, it should be added that we mean the fact that certain arguments are valid because of their form alone. To take an example, it may be said that if X contains Y, and Y contains Z, then X contains Z, i.e. X contains Z regardless of what X and Z are. It does not matter whether they are tins, hollow spheres or boxes within boxes, it is true to say that if X contains Y and Y contains Z, then X *necessarily* (as it is said) contains Z. Similarly, $1+1=2$, $2+1=3$, $2+2=4$, and so on, by virtue of the rules of arithmetic alone. This presents no difficulty for Super-Cedric, and even Cedric can make inference by the associative process which says A is followed by B, in its experience, and therefore given A, B follows.

We can also think of language from a literary point of view, where the language form is intended to convey feelings as much as rational descriptions, and this means that Super-Cedric should have the ability to describe its awareness of its internal states. But because it cannot point to them as it can to an external event, its meaning is sometimes more shadowy.

Human thought is embodied in words, and we cannot readily separate one from the other. The two views, held respectively by the scientific semanticists and the literary romantics, will differ in that they will each be concentrating primarily on different types of thinking: rational and logical thinking (maximum 'objectivity'); and everyday thinking about problems of people and their relationships (in practice, mixed 'objective' and 'subjective' thinking).

But, at this point, we can agree that the difference between these two types of thinking is, at most, a matter of degree. Differences in attitude to the significance of language will depend, in part, on a difference of view as to the nature of human thinking. So that, if it appears that thinking is a somewhat mysterious process, then it may also appear that language is mysterious, whereas if it is felt that thinking is a rational and scientifically explicable process to be learned like anything else, then language will similarly seem scientifically explicable.

In a sense, the distinction between rational and everyday thinking is justified by the existence of forms of communication as remote (or apparently remote) as poetry on one hand and mathematics on the other. We must continue to bear in mind these differences of modes of communication. It is not meant to imply that poetry is irrational, rather that it is not precise in the way that mathematics is, and uses references which are in many ways purely 'subjective'. In fact, as far as our machine offspring is concerned, we see that it is the 'internal' as opposed to the 'external' which is at issue.

Human language has slightly shadowy origins, but it might be guessed that it is some combination of grunts and groans (accompanied by gestures) and that the kind of noises made were limited by the functioning of the respiratory organs. No doubt gasping for breath or breathing heavily, or feeling pain and crying out, are the basic sounds which became stylized as phonemes from which words, and then sentences, came to be constructed. It is important to notice that a vital factor in communication is that it involves all the senses, but especially the visual and auditory.

The spoken word presumably came first, so that the auditory factor in language perhaps predominates over the visual, but the visual sense was just as important, perhaps even predominant, in the drawing and painting of pictures which are certainly used as part of the total communication process.

This is why, in the modern analysis of communication problems, the total communication process is analysed (pragmatics), where even the lifting of an eyebrow is important. The language and linguistic part of the communication can be abstracted from that total context if the need arises.

Alfred Korzybski was one of the first people to appreciate fully the vital importance of language to human beings. Without language people could not have accumulated information from generation to generation and as a result each species would have to start again, more or less from scratch; this, as was said earlier, is what he called 'time-binding'.

Language enabled us to accumulate knowledge. This was greatly speeded by the invention by Gutenberg of the printing press, later brought to England by Caxton. Communication was, after that, mainly through the printed word. But before that it was through the written word, and before that through the spoken word.

We know what we know by two methods. The first is by direct *acquaintance* with the environment (Cedric shows its registers) and the second is by *description* of the environment (Cedric says what the state of its registers is). We do not need to have been to Tahiti to know that Tahiti exists. This is just as well, otherwise many of us would have very small worlds indeed and the atlas (an important source of knowledge by description) would be useless. It is also the same with Cedric 2, who knows all about maze A from Cedric 1, although it has never seen it.

It can be seen that we have to symbolize sights and sounds so that a language which is basically made up of signs is also made up of symbols with which to carry the signs. This vital subject of language will be pursued somewhat further before the machines are shown at work using it. We should think initially of words and phrases as signs, and letters as symbols.

More precisely, signs are a class of inputs or stimuli (whether 'natural', like clouds; or man-made, like signposts) which refer to something (normally) other than themselves. Signs are signs for particular people if they act as pointers or routes (or parts of routes) to goals. Clearly signs may have 'private' significance (a tap on your partner's foot under the card table!) and indeed anything can be a sign of anything else for some person in some circumstances; this is the very essence of pragmatics (the study of the whole behavioural context of communication). We think of dictionary definitions as signs, and symbols, with publicly agreed definitions. We can be more precise about these definitions and say that the most frequently occurring types substitute a single term for a whole phrase. So, in a modern computer, you can nearly always substitute words for such phrases when the computer is used as a 'word processor'.

In the case of language signs, commonly called lansigns, symbols are used to make up the signs which are obviously conventional in the way that signposts are, rather than 'natural' as in the case of lightning signifying thunder. The symbols used are, of course, a, b, c . . . in English and they are put together to make up a language under the control of fairly complicated, although by no means complete or precise, rules of syntax.

Sometimes the word 'signal' is also used to represent a (symbolic) sign that has a wholly standardized meaning. Animals use signals which are natural, in their development, but symbolic in that they are associated with certain events by some sort of convention. They are signals in that they have, or should have, a fairly standard effect on the recipients. One can imagine Super-Cedric using words and then substituting words for phrases (definitions) and using a signal (e.g. help!) for generalized, and usually emergency, situations.

It seems reasonable to insist that a language must have some sort of grammatical rules, and must involve symbols and not be merely a collection of signs and symbols. This is because statements involving random collections of words will not be intelligible; rules of grammar, which involve the division of a sentence into subject and predicate, and each into nouns, adjectives, verbs, etc, coupled with rules of meaning – all incomplete in natural languages like English – are necessary to make for sensible discourse. This means that languages like English, French, German are obviously within this 'definition'. But so also are more formal languages, like Boolean algebra, or arithmetic, and computer languages such as ALGOL, COBOL and FORTRAN. In fact, the rules of the formal languages are precise and complete. The very existence of such computer languages for conventional computing purposes makes our task much easier.

The difference between these two sorts of language is that one has arisen as a result of evolution over thousands of years, and the other may have been constructed overnight. The difference is not necessarily of importance to Cedric, but it at least suggests that one should look at the evolution of languages, if only to see how they started.

Language probably began to emerge, as a language, as people moved from the use of the spoken to the written word. The whole question of how the use of primitive sounds led to a systemic use of sounds is a matter for some considerable controversy. One theory is that all sounds were imitation of animal sounds or natural sounds, and that most words were onomatopoeic; for example, Cedric might learn to use words like 'hum' to imitate the sound of its own power source.

The development of language in the individual is another aspect of the subject. It may be that the child (or so it has been suggested) reproduces the whole history of linguistic evolution, starting from primitive cries which are quickly satisfied by food and change of nappies; this is an example of the principle of reinforcement at work, as with Cedric, no longer hungry after eating. Then, gradually, the symbols and their referents are learned and statement formats and grammatical forms appreciated; all this is achieved by sound and by word of mouth, before anything is written or read. This is reminiscent of maturation and reminds us that real nervous systems have to grow to their eventual size: this is not true of readymade machine systems.

I should mention here the existence of theories that suggest that grammar is in some sense universal, and that particular grammars are variants of this universal grammar. The child, having inherited some sense of the universal grammar, has the problem of establishing only the detailed differences which mark off the particular grammar he is learning to use from all the possible ones.

Whether this argument for the existence of a universal grammar is or is not so, one may guess that the most general rules obviously come first, and progress is made later from these general rules to the particular syntactical details. None of this is important to Super-Cedric, unless it is insisted that Super-Cedric cannot be taught grammar (of a suitable computer language) but has to learn for itself.

The physiological basis of language certainly involves at the very least talking and hearing. Talking involves the complex use of the larynx, throat and breathing apparatus as well as the brain. Hearing involves senses, the physical vibrations of the air, first in the outer ear and then in the middle ear which transmits the vibrations mechanically to the inner ear; this stimulates the auditory nerve, and this in turn stimulates the auditory sections of the brain. I shall start by discussing the common features of both talking and hearing, and this at the level of the brain itself.

There are, of course, many areas of the brain which are specially concerned with language. Broadly speaking, the visual speech area is in that part of the brain concerned with vision, and the auditory speech area is in the part of the brain concerned with hearing. There is little doubt that the capacity to see and hear words and sentences has gradually emerged from the capacity to see and hear anything at all. In the same way as seeing and hearing in general involve recognition and understanding, so seeing and hearing words involves, as it were, the decoding of their 'meaning'. There are in existence, as I have said, many automatic (metallic) speech recognition systems and one could be built into Super-Cedric. Perhaps the best known is SID III, made at the National Physical Laboratory at Teddington in England.

The motor speech area of the brain is concerned with the actual utterance of the sounds which make up the speech. Once more, this is a rather specialized centre which has apparently emerged in the brain during the course of evolution. It is one of many such centres which have a relatively specific function in controlling the body's physical actions. Again we find a speech synthesizer in existence (one is made by ICL) which would allow Super-Cedric to speak, even if it still sounds a little like the voice of certain types of talking weighing-machine. It will not take long to 'humanize' Super-Cedric's voice, nor is this really relevant to the main quest for artificial intelligence.

From the point of view of the brain's function, the whole

subject of language is very complicated, and it is not my intention in this book to discuss every aspect of these complex features. What will be mentioned, however, are some of the features which are directly relevant to the understanding of how language can be used, by our copying method, in Cedric or more especially in Super-Cedric.

All that needs to be said about the purely neurological factors is that the brain acts as a storage centre, probably acting in a hierarchical fashion, within which hierarchy the ability to abstract and to generalize and to utilize information is a permanent process, and it is especially these abilities which are essential to effective thinking.

Information is fed into the sensory system, into the sensory parts of the brain, and information is fed out through the motor parts of the brain. So the brain specifically stores information which is fed in through hearing (including hearing spoken words) and seeing (including seeing written words) and the association centres of the brain are responsible for the processes of recognition which are so closely bound up with the 'meaning' of language. This starts as 'sounds' (the equivalent of X and Y) and finishes up with meanings.

To return now to a description of linguistic behaviour, we can regard language from the point of view of the introspective philosopher, or we can regard it from the point of view of the public observations of the scientist, as well as the poet, the politician, the lawyer, indeed Uncle Tom Cobleigh and all. It is the scientific technique with which we are concerned, and the one that has been most recently developed.

Philosophers have been responsible for dividing our universe sometimes into the physical and the mental, and this is not merely a matter of chance but is dependent in part on the very words we use in the first place, together with the fact that once a distinction of a verbal kind is made it is often assumed that this necessarily implies an equivalent distinction at non-verbal levels. It is precisely this point which presents a barrier to seeing Cedric (and, ironically, Super-Cedric even more) as having a mentality of its own. It may seem a curious reversal of the proper order of things that we would have said that our language has led to theories about the physical world. That language has often taken precedence over the observational powers which should lead to language, is undoubted. But to some extent this is a function of an unconscious process. Indeed, it should be expected that our languages will influence our scientific theories, just as our scientific theories influence language. I shall mention just one example of the interrelatedness of science (knowledge) and language. If I say, 'The world is square' (we seem often to talk in two-dimensional terms about a three- or even four-dimensional world) you cannot know for certain whether or not I am mistaken about the facts. Do I really regard the world as having a certain rectilinear shape? Or am I misusing the word 'square'? Either could be the case, so we can easily imagine the same sort of confusions occurring in the construction of science, at least parts of which are verbal models of reality. These are the sort of difficulties which occur when two Super-Cedrics talk to one another. It is interesting that this difficulty would be obviated if they were both remotely controlled by the same brain. Language is only required when two separate brains need to communicate. Of course, what I am saying is that if we make two Super-Cedrics into one, linguistic problems vanish.

Experimental psychologists in recent years have defined language as the medium for the expression of images and ideas which imply a kind of mental process, and it is only lately that they have come around to thinking of linguistic behaviour, like all other aspects of behaviour, as explicable in more mechanistic or behaviouristic terms.

A child starts to produce simple noises which are soon interpreted by parents or guardians as signs of affection and recognition, and the result of this sort of process is that parents feel that the existence of sounds, interpreted as part of their own language, implies an understanding of what those sounds or words mean. The suggestion is that the existence of a word implies a clear concept; this is not necessarily the case.

In children, the identification of words and objects observed represents an extremely primitive approach to language. But the fact remains that, to a child, words and sounds seem to be as much a part of an object, or a system, as its colour or its shape. They literally identify words and objects, or whatever the name we use for the vast and varied collection of things that words stand for, refer to, denote, connote or signify. All this is precisely what semantic and pragmatic analysis is designed to avoid.

I shall very briefly consider the question of language in lower animals (Cedric is in mind as a sort of lower animal). Animals can respond to linguistic signs; cats can learn to go into their feeding boxes when they hear some appropriate signal. This is ordinary conditioning, of course, in which the distinctive signs may happen to be verbal but have meaning (in the richest sense) only to the human observer. It might even be said here that they have a more precise meaning to the human observer, although they clearly also have some meaning for the animal.

Animals can display symbolic processes, as has been noted in sign learning or secondary reward training, for example, apes working for poker chips. Higher animals make use of memory in delayed reaction situations, and it can also be shown that some animals can represent objects to themselves, by images in memory. For example, a monkey was trained to wait blindfold through a delay period and then choose between one of two cups under which a food reward had been hidden. Sometimes, when the monkey was blindfold, a lettuce was substituted for a banana which had been hidden while the animal watched. When released, the monkey turned over the correct cup and extended his hand for the food, but when he saw it, he would not touch it; instead he would search about, showing signs of extreme surprise and irritation, and reject the lettuce entirely. He would, of course, always eat the lettuce whenever it was the food he expected.

There is no doubt that animals communicate with one another. Colonies of monkeys use a variety of signals in their natural habitat; certain cries by 'lookouts' seem to produce flight, and other sorts of characteristic social activity. The sounds do not appear to be wholly intentional communication, but rather to represent momentary emotional states, and this again underlines the origins of language as an outward expression of inward physiological conditions. The listening animal responds in terms of the state expressed, perhaps through identification, possibly due to the sound's quality being similar to that produced by the listening animal when in the same state.

One question is, how is it that human beings alone have developed language? The chimpanzee is capable of making thirty-two different speech sounds, and is also capable of distinctly representing objects in its environment; it can learn by observation and insight. None, however, of the various attempts to teach chimpanzees to speak has been really successful. Why is man the only animal capable of speech? We can only guess at the reasons: the development of language requires a sufficiently elaborate vocal mechanism, sufficient complexity of brain development to establish and maintain a mass of fine discriminations, and a cultural standardization to enable transmission and elaboration of specific and distinctive symbolic reactions. But none of this is of concern to us, because we know how to build the capacity of speech into our machine species.

Before leaving speech, we should ask ourselves more explicitly about the theories as to its origin. There are, broadly speaking, four such theories. The first is called the 'ding-dong' (mystical) theory, which assumes that certain objects have the power to evoke certain sounds from man. Once these sounds have been made in association with experiencing the object, the sounds come to mean the objects. The 'bow-wow' (imitative) theory assumes communication began by man's imitating sounds made by animals and things. Words such as 'buzz', 'rumble' and 'bark' are suitable examples, and the theory states that the idea of thunder prompted the primitive man to point skyward and mouth 'rumble, rumble'. Starting here, man goes on elaborating and the results are standardized by cultural and social evolutionary processes. The third is the 'pooh-pooh' (interjectional) theory, which assumes that various unlearned, emotional vocal responses tend to occur in stereotyped situations, for example, experiencing bad taste or smell, 'ugh!'; sudden pain, 'ow!'; pleasant tastes, 'mmm!'; and so on. This third theory seems very little different in fact from the second.

After reviewing the foregoing theories, Edward Thorndike produced a fourth theory which he called the 'babble-babble' theory. Accepting the existence of social grouping among prehumans and the presence of natural objects, tools, playthings, etc, we assume that our man-apes developed memory-images, ideas and expectations concerning people and objects about them. We must also assume these man-apes experimented with their vocal apparatus much as the young infant spontaneously produces noises. Supposing an intelligent man-ape produces a certain noise or expression in a particular situation or circumstance, then it seems likely that other members of the group would imitate the sound in like circumstances; we may expect imitation to play a vital role in the development of language in any society.

Enough is enough. I have allowed myself more licence than usual in discussing language. This is simply and solely because, of all aspects of human behaviour, the linguistic is the most complex and the most distinctive. The subject of this chapter is so vast that it could easily have spread into several books.

Cedric has to learn by conditioning, in the same way as animals, to associate sounds and symbols with the events of its world. In other words, thirst, hunger, danger, food, drink, turn left, and all aspects of Cedric's world can be symbolized, and not only by words. X could just as easily stand for thirsty, Y for hungry, and so on. In fact, of course, the words 'thirsty' and 'hungry' are used.

It has already been said that natural language has grown up over a very long period of time, and the only reason for Cedric to use the English language is if it wishes to talk to English people. As soon as we remove that constraint, Cedric can use any language it likes. In the man-machine communication world of tomorrow, some compromise between English and a computer language is highly probable.

In practice it is inevitably Super-Cedric who comes into serious contention when the question of language arises. We can tackle Super-Cedric exactly as we would a digital computer; it is, after all, a digital computer disguised as 'human'.

A computer uses a language such as COBOL (a business-oriented language) because it is fairly easy for a human being to learn and is also easy to translate into the computer's internal language (his so-called machine-code language) and by COBOL we can program the computer. I am talking now in terms of a very large computer, programmed interactively and capable of self-programming, where self-programming means writing a program which includes statements which, when completed, interactively rewrite the existing program. The essential feature of COBOL is that the computer translates instructions in a program in COBOL language into a machine-code instruction. So, to take a very trivial example: MULTIPLY 20 BY 3, and this gives 60, is something which is translated into the movement of several switches of our Boolean kind. The result is like a cyclometer or any meter that ticks up 20, three times, and the result (if we start from zero) is 60 'on the clock'.

It is clear that we have here at least a close analogy between COBOL language and machine-code language on the one hand and English and the binary code of the nervous system on the other.

Only one two-pronged problem remains for Super-Cedric and that is to translate COBOL into English, and make the machine code identical with the 'nervous system'. Since our main problem is synthesis rather than simulation (end-product rather than means) we will settle for simply translating COBOL into English. This is not too difficult; since, unlike COBOL, English does not have a completely precise syntax, we can leave a certain area of vagueness.

It can now be seen that to get Super-Cedric to talk is easy, because the human need to talk to computers has led us to construct convenient computer languages for ourselves. The interesting thing is that most of the complexities of language centre on the enormous difficulty human beings encounter in learning to use language, and the comparative simplicity we meet in handing it on.

Much existing philosophy is involved with language, and we meet problems over meaning (to decide in essence what words and statements refer to and in what way they refer) and truth (how to define our concept of a true statement and to know how it refers to reality). A muddle occurs in English, unlike COBOL and computer languages, because it has no complete set of rules, and as a result words used are often underdefined and their meaning is left to be made clear by the context in which they are used. Existing computers, working *algorithmically*, would find this difficult. They would need to take a *heuristic* view of language, and that is exactly what human beings do.

Super-Cedric, it need hardly be said, has the capacity to learn new words to add to its vocabulary, and so even if it started with COBOL it would soon add to COBOL vocabulary and also to COBOL operations. So it is that new nouns and verbs are added to the machine language and all the other parts of speech are more or less fixed (but could be added to if required).

The use of language in our machine depends upon one set of switch states, which are then used as symbols to refer to another set of switch states which are used as concepts and refer to all aspects of the learned environment. So if A leads to B, then both A and B are represented in Super-Cedric, and also 'A' and 'B' which are associated specifically with A and B by designation. This means that they are associated and, although it is a functional association unlike the other association in Super-Cedric, they have probability 1, or in other words they are an association which is fixed. We could always call cats 'dogs' and vice versa, but the change would certainly take time to get used to. In the human brain the symbol switch set is in one hemisphere of the brain and the other concept set in the other hemisphere.

All learning, and this is central to all thinking, depends upon association, and the simplest association is that of 'occurring together'. If rain occurs one hundred times and is recorded, and black clouds occur on ninety-nine of those one hundred occasions, then we associate the two, and the events are simply counted and stored. We will then assume that black clouds are a sign of rain (or in other circumstances we might say black clouds cause rain or even rain causes black clouds: a problem in itself).

Counting can now be added to the various important processes necessary to machine intelligence. Classifying, sorting (discrimination in perception and recognition), associating and naming (or labelling) are clearly other essential processes. The result of language in a society is that each member of that society has two partial models of the whole environment, and they are both symbolic, in form, inside the nervous system. One of the models translates into language for communication and the other into images and concepts which represent the outside world and to which the linguistic model also refers. It all sounds rather complicated but it is not really so. All that matters is that Super-Cedrics in their Super-Cedric society can talk and write, and must do so, since otherwise they would have no hope of survival.

5 The Machine as Scientist

How can his knowledge protect his
desire for truth from illusion?

W. H. Auden, *For the Time Being*

Perhaps we should now take stock of where we are. The machine being made, and the words 'being made' can if one likes now be construed as 'for which one is writing a program', is the one we have called Super-Cedric. It is a large modern digital computer exiled to the laboratory. It is 'chairbound'; it does not get up and move around since it is very much overweight: it could be trundled around on wheels – or it could trundle itself – but there is no point. There is no point because it can operate at any distance from base through its various 'limbs'.

Even though computers are becoming more and more powerful and also becoming smaller and smaller, there came a time in building logic boards into Cedric when we had to call a halt and say, as it started to slow down, that it could take no more. Like an overloaded car, it will gradually become more and more sluggish.

Cedric was never lost, but it was decided to leave its brain behind and operate by remote control. This new maze-runner, because it will be remembered that that is how it started out, could still become a super-brain, but on a different basis. This continuity is represented by calling Cedric 'Super-Cedric'.

In fact, the brain at home could control not just one, but many artefacts, and many other kinds of limbs besides. The brain at home also has the usual inputs available, in the form of punched card and punched tape and optical readers, and whatever else is needed. The latter are custom-made and are not generally available off the shelf.

The central processing is still the vital part where all the cognitive processes are, and these must, at the very least, include perception, learning, problem-solving, thinking and language.

Learning was illustrated, basically, in the case of Cedric's maze-running. It learned to run for food when hungry and drink when thirsty and later, with the addition of a few more logic boards, it could learn to run away from threats and dangers, and chase after prey. There is no question of its being able to learn without being motivated. In other words, to be goal-seeking is a basic requirement to learning, and the basic goals are wired in like *instincts*. The other goals are then acquired by association, as in conditioning. All our examples of conditioning in the previous chapter were also examples of learning.

Two points arise in our discussion. I use the vague label 'logic boards' for standard bits of computer equipment which simply switch information into different pathways, and are just like statements in Boolean algebra, either on or off, or 1 or 0; or, when we interpret such a system as a logic, true or false (we shall see more of this later). I should mention that Boolean algebra can be, and is, often used to describe electronic switching circuits, and as was said earlier, can be realized in hardware as AND-gates, OR-gates and NOT-gates.

The second point is quite different but of great importance. It is the principle of secondary motivation. This works as follows: if you go somewhere to eat, you satisfy a basic need and also enjoy the process because the restaurant is a good one. There are a whole series of events which are associated more or less closely with the main satisfaction, and these, as a result, acquire positive values. Everything else being equal, those events nearest in time to the satisfaction (or perhaps seen as most vitally connected, e.g. having enough money) are those which acquire the highest values. As we get older we prefer certain names and not others because we liked or disliked the people we have known with the same name. This is clearly another extension of Pavlov-type conditioning.

In practice, the hierarchy of motives (goals) is built up in terms of a whole set of positive and negative values, or valences as they are sometimes called, when out of context. A fried fillet of sole, for example, has a far greater (immediate) value when you are hungry than it does after a meal, but the valence (the shop or restaurant price) is more or less independent of whether or not the purchaser has just eaten: hence the distinction between value and valence.

What we have in Super-Cedric is a very complex set of associations built up through experience, and the associations are so tenuous that it is not always possible to discover what makes it like this and dislike that: the same is true for all of us.

In machine terms we can illustrate the principle of secondary motivation in terms of our logic boards and stores. Computer stores, incidentally, can take many forms: magnetic drums, magnetic tapes, magnetic cores, chemical processes, switching systems, and others besides: some slow (and usually cheap) and some fast (and usually expensive). The object is to put information in store and take it out again quickly. These stores are the equivalent of human memory. The fast memory is where information is stored while processing takes place, and is clearly closely connected with consciousness.

Now the information – which is wired-in to Super-Cedric – takes up locations in store. It can be thought of as a set of inputs $I_1, I_2, I_3 \ldots$ and a set of outputs $O_1, O_2, O_3 \ldots$

We have it wired so that we get connections between inputs and outputs such as I_1O_3, I_2O_2, I_3O_8, $I_4O_7 \ldots$ We can clearly have more tenuous connections, where the output is connected to the input *on condition* that something else happens. This we can write I_5O_6 IF M_2 (where IF means 'if and only if'), which says 'when you see a drink, drink it if and only if you are thirsty'.

Now the secondary-motivation principle throws up a whole set of inputs $J_1, J_2, J_3 \ldots$ which are part of the chain of activities I_5O_6. This, in ordinary terms, means that when thirsty I cannot immediately drink, but must go to the cupboard, pick up a glass and uncork the bottle (these are the Js); and now the process of going to the cupboard, picking up the glass, etc, are all (provided the drink is pleasant) given a positive value.

In our record in store we could add a value v to each connection, so that we have $I_1O_3(v)$, $I_2O_2(v) \ldots$ and then through secondary motivation we get $I_5K_7J_1K_2J_2K_3J_3O_6$ and the Js and Ks (the latter are responses to inputs) become v_7, v_8, v_9, or $+6$, $+8$, $+12$; and if the drink had been medicine, -6, -8, -12.

This could easily be built into Cedric and it would then learn to respond to other features of its environment in a positive or negative way by virtue of this principle of association. This is the very essence of learning, and depends upon a set of Boolean

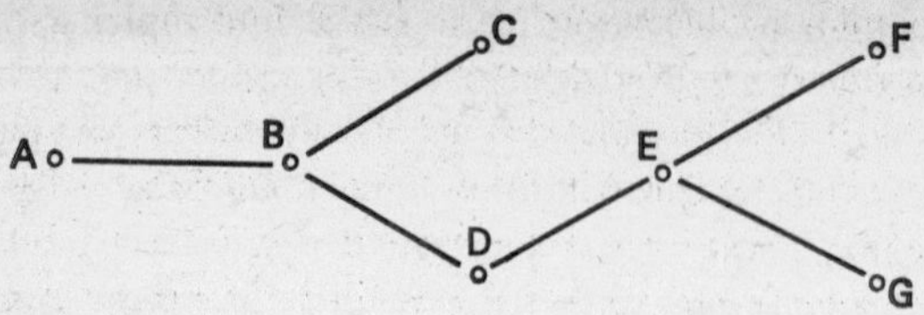

$A \rightarrow B \equiv D'$
$B \rightarrow C$
$B \rightarrow D \equiv C'$
$D \rightarrow E$
$E \rightarrow G \equiv F'$
$E \rightarrow F \equiv G'$

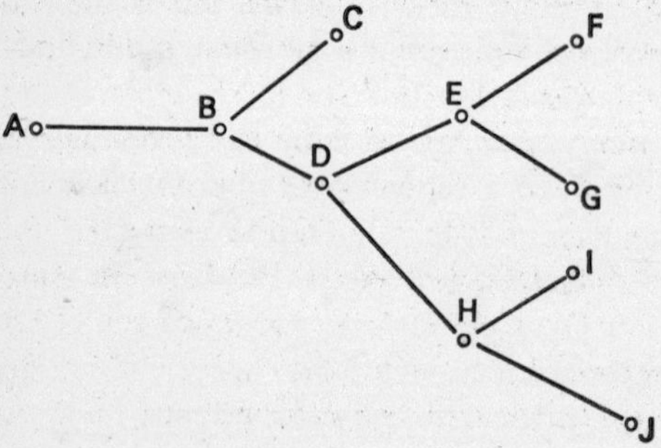

$A \rightarrow B$
$B \rightarrow D \equiv C'$
$B \rightarrow C \equiv D'$
$D \rightarrow E \equiv H'$
$D \rightarrow H \equiv E'$
$H \rightarrow I \equiv J'$
$H \rightarrow J \equiv I'$

If we reinforce the 'correct' route we get:

$A \rightarrow B \rightarrow D \rightarrow H \rightarrow J$

if J is the goal.

Figure 1
Two conditional probability 'mazes' made up of Boolean two-choice points.

switches wherein any degree of complexity can be reduced to go or no-go (1 or 0).

The platform is now set for all the higher cognitive activities. Problem-solving can be seen as a type of learning which is specific and aimed at bridging some sort of knowledge gap. When Cedric starts to run a new maze, it learns to solve the problem of how to get to the goal, whatever that goal may be.

More complex problem-solving is geared into thinking, which in turn is geared into language.

When we tackle thinking, we necessarily tackle concepts and their formation. When talking of human thinking we talk of concepts like classes: the concept of redness or red, roundness or round, and so on. In Cedric or Super-Cedric the concepts are the state of the switches. In humans the concepts are the same: the state of the 'switches' in the nervous system.

The nervous system is in fact a complex Boolean switching system and this is the point noticed by the pioneers of cybernetics – Norbert Wiener and his associates – back at the beginning of World War II. This still leaves problems. For example, is the mind the operation of the brain? Is the whole of the brain basically a very complicated version of Cedric? In other words, did the whole thing really evolve from Cedric-like beginnings? I think the answer to all three questions is yes, but the answer I would give would not vary very much even if some parts of the human nervous system were non-Boolean. However, we must return to our task of mapping out the machine which will be the prototype of the new species.

Concepts are formed by switches being thrown, and the word can be taken to represent a switch state. We now build language to represent concept as labels represent events: 'Chicago' designates or labels Chicago. The single quotation marks indicate the word, thus "'Chicago' has seven letters" and "Chicago has a harbour" are correct, whereas "Chicago has seven letters" and "'Chicago' has a harbour" are nonsense.

Now look briefly at the human brain. It has a store (however constructed) which distinguishes short-term from long-term memories. The basis on which memories are kept, thrown away or rejected is at least the following: recency (recent events are best remembered), frequency (the more often events occur, the more likely they are to be remembered) and value (certain things are obviously more important than others). Examples of value are obvious: it is easier to remember the birth of your own child twenty years ago than having burnt the cabbage one day five years ago. Another fact about memory is that where muscular coordination skills are involved, as in riding a bicycle, there seems to be very little chance of forgetting.

All this sort of information can, in the same way, be placed in a computer store and retrieved as required. This is a very simple part of the operation; but we do have to think about how we create new concepts, and the simplest way is to use our old friend Boolean algebra. By taking concept A and concept B, we quickly arrive at concept C where $C = A \cap B$.

You could say that the concept 'round red object' is obviously not a primitive concept, but this is not quite so obvious when you remember that even so-called primitive concepts can be broken down into sub-concepts, so red at one level is a compound of wavelengths and frequencies, particles and waves. But in case it should be thought that this is cheating, it must be remembered that all concepts which are new to us are in fact only understood in terms of what is already familiar.

If Jack comes in and tells us he has seen some quite new animal (new to us, anyway) and says, 'I've seen a corty', we ask: 'What is a corty?' (We suspect we may have misheard the word 'corgi', but what is so special about seeing a corgi?) He then can only explain that a corty is a five-legged cat. This gives us a new, you will notice conjoint (or compound), concept. In future we might ourselves say to someone else, 'I've just seen a borty', and in case you have never seen a borty, let me explain that it is a longer, thinner version of a corty. Then everyone is happy, and remains happy as long as our descriptions and definitions are couched in terms of concepts which are already familiar.

So concepts can be built up, and new ones stored, as a result of our experience. This means that had Cedric the storage space (as Super-Cedric has) it could build up a whole set of features that occurred to it: three-dimensional maze (therefore two-dimensionality, dimension, two, and by implication all numbers), stairs, up, down and so on. It can easily be seen how Cedric's environment could soon become enormously complicated, and if it had the storage space, then there is no need to restrict it to the simple mazes with which it started.

Any machine that can discriminate between X and Y, blue and red, say, must have the concept of 'blueness' and 'redness'. This does not in any sense need to be a conscious process, although in human beings it will often be so. More complicated concepts can, as we have said, be built up in terms of these primitive concepts.

The only reason you can be sure that a machine has the conceptual capacity is by the way it behaves. It is the chestnut of 'Other Minds' once more. You assume your friends are conscious because they behave as if they were. Similarly you assume black box A is the same as black box B if it behaves identically under all circumstances.

It should be said again here that there is a difficulty in knowing the internal state of any system. If we treat it as a black box and do not open it, this makes it difficult to know how to control it, or stop its manufacture. By the phrase 'knowing the internal state', we mean either 'not opening the black box' or, equally, opening it and not knowing how to interpret what we see.

The plot thickens, but our knowledge of how to understand it is enormously increased. We now have a system for generating our internal model of the external world – we sometimes call it a conceptual model – and like a map of territory we can make it as complicated as we need, or as circumstances demand.

This means that the sort of conceptual world that Super-Cedric has is bound to involve consciousness, since the ability to conceptualize all external events as well as internal events demands the use of the word 'I', and at this point the whole process of self-reference becomes a reality.

Now we come to a consideration of Super-Cedric in action. How do we put its rational side to the test? There is no better test than to say, 'This is scientific method in action', and then to ask: 'Can Super-Cedric be a scientist?' The answer is yes, but first we must look at scientific method in action.

Science involves the process of collecting facts, and although it is certainly true that fact-collecting plays an important part in science, it is by no means the whole of it. Just as important as fact-collecting is the setting up of theories, theoretical structures, models, etc, which allow the use of both *deductive* and *inductive logic*. What we must now do is to go over each of the various steps involved in the total scientific process, explaining each as far as is necessary for an understanding of what science entails, while having in mind the problem of computerization, or in particular how it works for Super-Cedric.

In talking of scientific method we are taking only a global or broadbrush look at the process, and it does not by any means follow from this that any particular scientist at any particular time is involved in the whole of this global process. The chemist doing experiments in his laboratory, or the biologist inspecting tissue under a microscope, may be involved in only a small part of the total activity of theory-construction and logical reasoning, although often he is more involved than he might appear to be at first sight, even to himself. Of course, there is still a lot of debate as to the detail of scientific method, but this is not relevant to our argument here.

Many books on logic and scientific method have been written about the detail of the subject: how hypotheses are confirmed under certain restricted conditions, and precisely what sort of experimental controls are suitable for some set of observations, and all these techniques are perfectly possible for Super-Cedric to carry out, if it can deal with the general procedures.

Scientific procedures can be thought of in terms of two principal operations: deductive and inductive. These operations can occur in either order and therefore we can arbitrarily select the deductive procedure first for discussion. A set of assumptions, whether these be set out explicitly, as postulates in a formal system such as Boolean algebra, or whether they be implicit and merely stated in ordinary language, or indeed whether they be in some sort of symbolic form, as in chemistry, represent the starting-point for the making of deductive inferences. This is something which can be performed with Boolean algebra, and by interpreting the classes as propositions we can construe Boolean algebra as a propositional logic: a logic which deals in the statements or sentences of ordinary English.

In the case of human beings, a deductive inference is usually based on the language used to describe that part of the system in which we are interested. It is obvious that science is partitioned into various sub-departments, all of which are a part of the totality of human knowledge, but nevertheless are somewhat specialized, and are often thought of under their well-known specialized names of chemistry, physics, etc. We are not concerned with these distinctions here.

The deductive process is one of drawing logical inferences from the assumptions, and from this we generate further statements, sometimes called theorems in a formal (axiomatic) system, which apply to the system being described. Deduction itself is a symbolic process, and refers to the conclusions which follow from the assumptions. A simple logical deduction is one of the kind: 'If I am in Salisbury, and Salisbury is in Wiltshire, then it follows (deductively) that I am in Wiltshire.' This is an obvious deductive inference, sometimes called a logical inference, and one we can draw in most cases without much difficulty. Unfortunately, some deductive inferences are made in much more complex circumstances than these, and some which appear genuine at first sight turn out to be fallacious.

To look at a slightly more complicated example: if there are 366 people in a particular room at a particular time, and we overlook leap year, then it follows that at least two people in that same room must have the same birthday. This is true because we can allocate 1 January to one, 2 January to another, 3 January to another, right through to 31 December; and after we have exhausted the 365 days and allocated them to 365 people, we are left with a 366th person, and since we have agreed to ignore leap year, there *must* be a duplicate birthday. This is not necessarily asserting anything about the factual situation, of course, because it may be that all the 366 people were born on the same day. All it is asserting is that certain things must necessarily follow by virtue of the way the problem is posed.

It will be noted in our more complex example of deduction that it was dependent on the semantics of the situation: this is because we have rules of meaning (designation or interpretation) to add to our symbols A, B, C . . . as would appear in Boolean algebra. If the word 'birthday' meant the hour in which you were born instead of the day on which you were born, then the argument would fail. We should remind ourselves once more that arguments can be formal as opposed to factual, as in the case of the one about birthdays. That is, if we say a implies b and b implies c, then a implies c in a formal argument, in that it is true whatever a, b and c are, such that the implication is transitive in the way suggested. It is obviously true that 'If Salisbury is in Wiltshire and I am in Salisbury then I am in Wiltshire', is of the form a implies b and b implies c and therefore a implies c, whereas the argument 'I am the father of x and x is the father of y so I am the father of y' clearly does not follow in the same way.

So we must be careful to fit our formal models to our 'factual' theories, like maps to territory.

One clearly has to be careful about using formal arguments for factual information which does not have the same structure as the formal structure (maps must fit territories). Equally, in any sort of factual discussion one has to be careful about fallacious arguments (paradoxes). Thus we may find examples like, 'The barber in the village shaves everyone except those who shave themselves'; if we ask who shaves the barber, the answer cannot sensibly be given because the argument has been stated paradoxically, which suggests that he both shaves and does not shave himself at the same time. We have, of course, excluded the possibility, by implication, of his being bearded (or of not being 'he' at all!) and recognize merely that certain apparently valid arguments can often cloak logical fallacies.

So much, then, for deduction, which is the process of drawing out, by logical argument, what is inherent in a set of assumptions, which may be formal and concerned only with the structure of the argument, or may be factual and concerned with the semantics, i.e. the meaning of the terms being used.

Whatever the deductive procedure involved, the result is a set of factual statements about that part of the world which as scientists we are trying to describe, and these factual statements can be the source of observation designed to test their accuracy. It is true that either the assumptions, or the statements which follow logically from the assumptions, can be tested for their empirical veracity. Obviously science is concerned with collecting true statements, whether they are particular or general, and the point about scientific method is to try to discover whether or not a statement is true. If Cedric 1 says to Cedric 2, 'Maze A is identical with maze B', it is easy enough for Cedric 2 to check this by running maze B as if it were maze A and finding that it does not work, i.e. the statement is not true.

In a sense, the process of observation is the most characteristic of scientific processes, since it is systematic observation, and this includes experimentation, which one thinks of most readily when one thinks of practical science. The fact that the observations might be well controlled, either by the design of the experiment, or by the use of suitable statistical controls, or by suitable apparatus to isolate certain variables, or by increasing the power of observation by a microscope or telescope, does not matter. It does not in any way alter the fact that observation is the critical method by which the truth of statements is tested.

It should be noted that scientific explanation is akin to this descriptive process, where by 'explanation' we mean the use of general laws (or hypotheses) from which particular explanatory descriptions can be derived. Such explanations presuppose causal relations of whatever complexity existing in our domain of interest - Super-Cedric.

The question which is paramount at this point concerns the computerization of the deductive process, and that has already been done, since Boolean algebra and other such logical systems in various forms can easily be shown to work on the computer. Our realization that deduction can be computerized depends not only on the evidence of a large amount of work which demonstrates the point, but on the principle which derives from the work of a group of mathematicians to the effect that 'all finite games have an algorithm'.

By 'finite games' we mean all games, or processes, which can be completed in a finite number of steps, and this includes chess, by virtue of the rules. By an algorithm (or decision procedure) we mean an automatic procedure requiring no insight or intelligence and akin to the word 'computerizable' in the most limited sense of that word. All finite games and the whole of deductive arguments may not be quite the same, but are near enough so for our purpose. Therefore we know beyond doubt that Super-Cedric can perform deductive logic.

The second aspect of scientific method, which will be used to test Super-Cedric, starts with observation and goes through a process known as induction, sometimes called inductive logic, to arrive at generalizations which are the hypotheses which are broken down into assumptions and form the starting-point for deduction. We generalize by saying that if a_1 implies b_1, and a_2 implies b_2, etc . . . then all a's imply b's. We could write this simply as A implies B. Such a generalization could be made by Super-Cedric if, for example, *all* mazes started with a left turn.

The process of induction is that of generalizing from the

particular, and is therefore in some sense the opposite of deduction, which is particularizing from the general. Like deduction, induction is dependent on language, since knowledge can hardly be thought of as knowledge unless it is communicable and therefore capable of being stated in some sort of language, whether symbolic or otherwise. It has the added ingredient, in the case of induction, of being factual.

The basis on which the generalizations are made is observation: Cedric's two sensors could be enough. This is an important point, because of course deduction can cater for statements which refer to nothing in reality at all: this is what we meant by separating X, Y, Z . . . as formal symbols from their use as words to describe things. This is a thread that comes up again and again and runs throughout our analysis. It can always be remembered by the analogy: 'Maps can and must be distinguished from the territory they map.'

An inductive argument could be of the form: 'I have seen one swan and it is white, I have seen two swans and they are both white, I shall then assume that all swans are white.' We are very careful to say, in making the inductive generalization, that a swan is defined independently of its colour, otherwise it would be *logically true* to say that swans are white, and anything that was in every other way a swan but some other colour than white would be regarded as 'not-a-swan'. It is clear that there is no point in making observations about things which are already logically or semantically determined (or defined). Scientific statements have to be testable. Another way of saying the same thing is to say that science deals only in statements which are capable of being confirmed or falsified. If it is impossible to invalidate a statement, it is not testable. This does not mean that we want to invalidate every statement, only that if it is not capable of being invalidated, it is not a factual statement. Science, of course, must be made up of factual statements, i.e. statements that describe some aspect or aspects of reality.

The difficulty with the inductive argument is that it is always, at best, probabilistic; we can never be sure that we have found a true inductive generalization. There is no way in which we can see all swans, or be sure that we have seen all swans, and if we take a typical logician's point of view, and talk about seeing all swans 'at all times t', which means all the past and all the future as well, then it is clearly impossible to confirm such a statement. But even if we take the present time alone, there is no way in which we can be sure that we have seen every swan, and as a result, of course, all factual statements can reasonably be said to be open to doubt; or, very simply, one could be wrong.

It should be noticed that the form of these factual statements is of the kind, 'if . . ., then – – –', where the first gap '. . .' is filled by the inductive generalization and the second gap '– – –' is filled by the deductive inference. These two interact sometimes in a haphazard way in scientific argument (indeed in all argument), but essentially it is the integration of inductive and deductive inference, coupled with systematic well-controlled observation, which provides the factual basis for scientific model- (map-)building.

It is more difficult to show that induction is computerizable, but even so we might reasonably argue that conditional probability machines, such as those developed by Albert Uttley, give one strong grounds for optimism. These say, once again, that 'if p occurs, q follows' and if this is true for all p's (say p_1, p_2 . . .), then we can say in general 'any p is followed by a q'. One can see the signs of maze-running again, where we *might* find that any left turn is *always* followed by a right turn. There is a branch of statistics with the ugly name 'stochastic processes' which deals with a series of symbols, so that we can map out the chances of any event occurring and when it is likely to occur. A really interesting point here is that we can make up English statements by just such a repetition of words on a frequency basis. This means a certain pattern of symbols could be detected as a frequently occurring English sentence. It is this sort of repetition that makes the decoding of coded messages possible, since we could pick up JKMPQ say, as 'I like running long mazes', if the frequency of symbols was correct for the equivalent words. We must remember this sort of *sequential system* of analysis.

When we talk about scientific model-building, we leave it free to the model-builder to use whatever building bricks he likes: words, symbols, pictures, anything can be used. The building bricks of numbers have led to mathematics, which is clearly applicable to a very large number of things where quantification (the use of numbers and numerical operations) applies. There is also a whole field of activity where one is more interested in relationships, particularly logical relationships, and where the development of logical models – like Boolean algebra – is more appropriate. There are further aspects of knowledge where chemical formulae have been more appropriate, and of course many aspects of knowledge where ordinary linguistic descriptions are more appropriate.

When we use the word 'mathematics' it is not meant to imply that mathematics is concerned *only* with numbers or quantification. Mathematics is not easy to define precisely, but much of mathematics has been concerned with number and the quantification that goes with number, and much of the world of physics, for example, has been amenable to that sort of descriptive model. But not all. Some parts of mathematics deal with physical relationships, logic or other precise statements which are not numerical. Mathematics is, of course, also a language, because it can be used for communication; and it is also precisely defined.

Model-building is essentially a scientific process, like the internal store of any of the Cedric family, and the interpretations we place on models (as has been made clear) make them into theories, just as we place a factual interpretation on formal symbols. This is how languages are made. The model is, in a sense, an abstract structure concerned with relationships and the like, whereas the definition and interpretation we place on the model makes it into a factual theory. This relationship between model and theory is rather similar to the relationship between induction and deduction, and, of course, between maps and territory.

We will now caricature the scientist. Suppose we have a visitor from another planet coming to Earth, one who has a good training in scientific method, and is therefore familiar with deductive and inductive inferences as well as systemic observation and well-controlled experiments. He is sent to Earth to try to find out, in some particular location, say Salisbury, what time the shopkeepers open their shops in the morning and what time they close them in the evening. He knows from the start that he can observe only so many shopkeepers, therefore he carries out what statisticians call a *random sample*.

He knows that he cannot ask questions of the shopkeepers because they may not tell him the truth; and since we are talking by analogy with science, a physicist cannot ask a particle he is observing what its velocity and position in space are, for obvious reasons. Therefore he arrives on Earth, sets up his observation post and observes, say on Monday morning, that the shopkeepers come at 9.00 a.m. and leave at 5.00 p.m. He observes the same on Tuesday and makes the obvious (and only possible) inductive inference that every day is the same. By deduction he then concludes that if every day is the same, tomorrow will be the same, therefore Wednesday also will be 9.00 a.m. to 5.00 p.m. He in fact finds that on Wednesday they work from 9.00 a.m. to 1.00 p.m. and therefore this invalidates his hypothesis, and he has to think of another one. He could then suggest that the repetition which he is looking for is exemplified by 9.00 to 5.00, 9.00 to 5.00, 9.00 to 1.00, and one sees very clearly at this point what science (and all objective analysis) is about. It is, wherever possible, about repetitive patterns which can be observed in the environment. Where we get precise repetition we call the system *deterministic*, and where we fail to find precise repetition which as in most actual cases (although we sometimes get fairly near to it) then we are talking about *statistical* systems. What of course is needed is the ability to forecast with respect to the repetitions.

Our observer returns on Thursday and finds that it is 9.00 to 5.00, and Friday is 9.00 to 5.00; so far so good, but on Saturday the shopkeepers work from 9.00 to 5.00 again, which upsets his hypothesis and creates gloom. But it is only a matter of time before he hits on a seven-day cycle, after observing that they do not turn up at all on Sunday. However, even this seven-day cycle is not wholly precise, as he discovers on the first Bank Holiday he reaches.

After several years in Salisbury (and it would take him that amount of time) he discovers that the cycle he is searching for is more nearly a 365-day cycle, but even this is not exactly accurate because Leap Year occurs every fourth year. This is a source of a great deal of confusion to him, because the first time he meets Leap Year he might easily think he has made a mistake in his counting. He will have to stay at least two Leap Years, probably three, before he begins to see that Leap Year is something which happens every fourth year: an extra day is put into 365, making a 366-day year.

In the end it can clearly be seen that the only useful material the visitor has acquired is something which could be the basis for a 'Visit Salisbury Bureau' to be set up on his own planet, and even this would be subject to error because he could not be sure, after he returns to his own planet, that things have not changed. When he said, 'Well, normally they open at 9.00 and close at 5.00, except on Wednesdays', this may no longer be true, since Salisbury may have decided to change its half-day. In the second place, of course, he would be giving only a statistical statement about what the majority of people do in Salisbury (or what the people do in Salisbury on the average), because all the people do not open and shut their shops at the same time. There are important exceptions, like off-licences, which require a special corollary to the general theory. Nor can he argue that what applies to Salisbury applies to any other part of England, unless he has actually observed other parts of England. Nevertheless, he is performing the vital and basic act of forecasting or predicting: it is this which is the essential part of our method.

The ability to generalize on data is only true to the extent that you have sampled the data in the first place; this is a basic principle of scientific method. So it can be seen from this that the scientist's role is a fairly complicated one, in which he has to be a statistician, a logician, a very careful observer and documenter of facts, and has also to have a great deal of common sense. Super-Cedric needs all these characteristics, and we can make sure it has them. All the statistical methods are readily usable by computers, and they could have been discovered from scratch by a computer which has a logical ability and can build up records and 'games' in its memory store.

What we have said about science is meant to be a straightforward account of the sort of steps needed to acquire information, which is as objective as we know we can get it. We accept the fact that we shall impose, as human beings, our own interpretations on the findings supplied by our observations, and our logic. We shall impose personal experience, hunch, flair and the like, and must inevitably do so whether we like it or not: all this (see also chapters 6 and 7) can be done by Super-Cedric.

We need to notice that Super-Cedric, armed with all this paraphernalia, can predict (here come the sequences and their record again), and, if it can generalize (this now means perform inductions), can also understand what happens around it.

Prediction is essentially the same as forecasting and involves knowing (or having *some* reason to believe), or even just believing, that if you market product X then it will be bought in sufficient quantities to justify the expense in producing it and in providing the necessary launching campaign. The main point of our methodology is to try to provide the evidence for having the reason to believe, rather than merely believing.

The difference between prediction and understanding is a matter of degree. If a doctor says, 'I give a patient medicine A for a spotty face and the spots go', then this entails a prediction, and if the occurrence predicted happens regularly, it becomes a good prediction, even though he may have no idea why medicine A has such an effect. All that matters is that it does have the desired effect. If now I find medicine A has the opposite effect on spotty hands (i.e. it makes them spottier) and I gradually accumulate more and more evidence, I can begin to formulate a theory as to why medicine A has the effect it has; and if this theory is highly confirmed, as in the case of our visitor to Salisbury from another planet, so the feeling of understanding begins, and so we will say in the end, if the theory seems to be correct, that we understand the use of medicine A. We mean that we have knowledge of a much greater range of predictability and have established the principles – the theory – on which the predictions are based. The same was true of Cedric's maze-running. The prediction was possible without understanding, but given the generalization to all mazes, the awareness and the understanding followed.

From our ability, ideally to understand, or, at the next best, at least to predict – and if not absolutely, at least better than chance – stems our ability to control. We are enabled to control those aspects of our environment covered by the theory – and the model or models.

Scientific method (and this is the mirror of our needed blueprint) is composed of a number of stages and we have emphasized some of them:

1. Collecting information (Super-Cedric perceiving).
2. Deductive (logic) reasoning (Super-Cedric using symbols inferentially).
3. Inductive (logic) reasoning (Super-Cedric building up evidence for its hypotheses).
4. Formulating hypotheses (Super-Cedric collecting or formulating hypotheses from concepts).
5. Deducing the consequences of the hypotheses (Super-Cedric making inferences again).
6. Testing the hypotheses (Super-Cedric perceiving again).

Now we merely add a few very important points by way of a reminder. The first is that, in effect, the centre of Super-Cedric's activities is a high-speed filing system (electronic, of course) in which the basic associations are set up and their occurrences counted. This set of sequences allows us to see how the causal connections are made in reality and how predictions and intelligent behaviour become possible.

The next point is of vital importance to remember all the time. Super-Cedric does not do merely what it was programmed to do. We program it in the general sense to collect information and use it (generalize on it, etc) to pursue its own goals. To play chess like a master implies that the programmer programs Super-Cedric to collect all the relevant data regarding the rules and strategies of chess and then allows it to fill up its storage registers with all the best sequences, king to KP4; WB to QP3 . . . and so on, just like maze-branches, and with games won or lost recorded. It learns for itself that by reading or playing (remember description or acquaintance) it can quite quickly beat the programmer.

A last point to ponder is that you cannot 'pull the plug out' on Super-Cedric. One thing you do when you manufacture an 'intelligent machine' is to ensure that, when it proceeds on its own, it quickly learns to stop you 'pulling out its plug'. You are then confronted by another 'human being'. You may try to starve 'him' or kill 'him', but 'he' will try to stop you and may retaliate.

The reasons for arguing that Super-Cedric is a completely

intelligent rational machine ('can be a scientist') is that it can collect data, and process data, which means perceiving and recognizing events; it can perform logical operations and use language to describe its external environment and its internal states. This is all that is required of a scientist, so Super-Cedric can certainly be a scientist. Indeed, in terms of what has been said about black boxes, it is clear that Super-Cedric could be a scientist without our even knowing it.

It all started with running mazes, but running mazes is a very much more universal activity than is obvious at first sight. Almost all other activities are maze-running in effect, either with reality or a symbolic version of reality (a map). This then involves the careful checking of the map with experience, and then our maze-running Cedric has become the scientist Super-Cedric. The jump may seem huge, but in terms of the underlying mechanisms it is not. It is much the same set of Boolean on-off processing, multiplied many hundreds of times.

We should emphasize that the practical reasoning used by Super-Cedric will in fact go wellbeyond classical logic, since it will be *purposive* (and not just permissive as in the classical forms).

Similarly our account of scientific method is limited to the simplest example of hypothetico-deductive method. Science deals with much more than this, since explanation can take care of non-periodic or partially periodic processes such as are embodied in a scientific study of history. We have inevitably supplied a simplified account of both logic and science.

6 Emotional Machines

Our rulers: politicians, 'diplomats', bankers, priests of every description, economists, lawyers, etc, and the majority of teachers remain at present largely or entirely ignorant of modern science, scientific methods, structural, linguistic and semantic issues . . ., and they also lack an essential historical and anthropological background, without which a sane orientation is impossible.

Alfred Korzybski, *Science and Sanity*

So far, so good! A clear picture is emerging of the rational capacities of man possessed by our machine. The phrases 'cold logic' and 'cold reason' are often rather amusingly used to describe the rational aspects of people's behaviour. The implication is that the humanity of people, their warmth and kindness, as well as their fear and hatred, stem from something rather more than logic and reason. There is some truth in this, in so far as people have a part of their nervous system and brain which is concerned with emotional activities and what in general we call conative behaviour.

It should just be added that the rough distinction between cognition and conation is between rational, logical and objective behaviour on the one hand, and emotional (often subjective) behaviour on the other.

I am following in this book the general practice of using terms which are normally used to describe human behaviour to describe Cedric and Super-Cedric and then asking about the extent to which the similarities hold, or the extent to which there is a justification for using the same term for both. In moving to a discussion of emotions we are moving further than before from the fairly obvious preserve of computers. Computers do not need to possess emotions to cope with arithmetic or logic, but do need them if they are to be groomed for independence. If emotions like pleasure and pain are not associated with activities, then a machine cannot be sure, any more than a human being can, of recognizing the pleasure in performing certain acts and the pain in performing others and, as a result, trying to avoid the latter.

If the organic processes are attuned to pleasure and pain, then the species acquires good survival values by tending to avoid death and to seek out food, drink and sex. The principle of secondary motivation is involved and this reinforces otherwise neutral events pleasurably (in the limit, ecstatically) and painfully (in the limit, agonizingly). From these beginnings stems all the emotive colouring which guides all our actions and presents us with our feelings and the physiological side-effects of laughing and crying.

Conative behaviour is usually contrasted with cognitive behaviour and it can be assumed that the two are intermingled in human behaviour, more often than not in an inextricable manner. We shall now look again at how human beings behave, and at how their biological systems operate.

I mentioned earlier that in the ordinary course of processing input information, whether the input just happens to occur and is recorded, or whether it has been actively sought out by the person concerned, the process is one of sensing the event and transmitting the fact through the internal system. Or more particularly, as in the case of a visual event, to have something impinge on the retina – perhaps first on the periphery, on the rods, and then centrally, on the cones – so that it is transmitted to the visual cortex of the brain where it is classified.

This is by no means a simple process, as some more biological 'accidents' are involved. The left half of each retina sends information to the left visual cortex and the right half of each retina to the right visual cortex. It should be explained that the brain itself is in two parts which are joined together. It looks indeed like a huge walnut, with each lobe of the walnut making up one half of the brain. The reason for this is the manner in which the nervous system evolved, and, in the brain structure which emerged, gave a continuity to the visual field and also facilitated binocular vision: the integrated vision of two eyes and the resultant ability to perceive depth.

The human eyes have rods at the periphery of the retina which record movement, and cones at the centre which record detail, for the human being receives emergency messages primarily from the rods and then a clear identification by the cones. The cones and rods are both involved in the straightforward (the letter) and the emergency (the telegram) messages. This much is certain, but the routes of the letter and the telegram are certainly different. The letter might be said to take the cognitive route and the telegram the conative route. We would indeed argue that the very emergence of man through the threat of extinction from rival species, shows that he could not have survived without both these capacities.

The emotions are connected to the alarm system in a fairly complicated manner. In the first place the human body is what is called homeostatic. It stabilizes its behaviour and acts in a manner designed to facilitate its primary needs at any particular moment. This means that in a state of fear or rage (and the effect is cognative, not cognitive) the person facilitates his organic state by automatically increasing the heartbeat and dilating the arteries to speed up the blood supply to the muscles. This happens in order to enable physical activity to take place with the minimum effort and in the minimum time. It is of no consequence whether the effort is to fight or to run away; the muscular needs are, in either case, much the same.

This toning-up, or preparing, of the body's internal state is made possible by what is called the autonomic nervous system. The autonomic nervous system is a part of the total nervous system, but is distinguished from it by concentrating its activities on the automatic control of all the so-called involuntary organs. This means the heart, lungs, liver, pancreas, kidneys, and all the organs of which you cannot say, 'I will have more of this now and less of that.' You can voluntarily control your breathing and hand movements, but not your kidneys' or your liver's activity: at least, not directly, unless you are a very unusual person.

There are two branches to the autonomic nervous system. One increases the activity of the organ under control and the other decreases it, and they act rather like the two reins on a horse. As it happens, they also operate by chemical means, but this we know is simply because the human machine is colloidal protoplasmic in its working. Just as our ordinary motor car uses petrol, and a steam engine depends on steam and an oil fire depends on oil, a human being, in turn, depends upon food and oxygen to make his internal mechanisms operate correctly.

It is not surprising, under these circumstances, that the internal organization of the human being is such a complicated morass of chemical and biochemical processes which analyse and synthesize various products to make nerves and muscles work effectively. Even the control side is partly chemical, as we know from the close association of the endocrine glands with the brain. The principal endocrine gland, the pituitary, is lodged in the brain itself.

So we have an automatic control system operating on the internal organs, which works in close connection with the central nervous system and the brain. The nature of the bodily emergency is given a sensible purpose by the brain itself. Consider a state of fear or rage. These are indistinguishable organically, since all the body understands is that there is a call to 'action stations'. The brain has recognized a threat or a prey and has gone through the processes of thought, which require that it consider how to escape or attack.

Examine the threat first. The considerations for escaping can easily be seen in Cedric's terms as a moving away from the threat to the remotest part of the maze, say, and hiding or circulating only as and when it is chased by what is now apparently a mobile threat – from another Cedriclike system from an enemy species, the obvious analogy with human society seen in its evolutionary context.

To achieve this end we should note that Cedric has now to be able to discriminate between threats and dangers as well as between thirst, hunger, turn right, etc. But it already has the maze-maps available and if it knows that the goal is escape, and this means hiding as far away as it can, and taking whatever evasive steps are necessary and possible, we have a clear idea of how Cedric needs to behave, and will behave.

Now to another example. If Cedric can discriminate between threats and preys, where indeed the prey may be to satisfy its hunger or where the prey is an enemy (i.e. a potential threat, in many cases), then the appropriate action is now to track and chase the prey. Once again it is armed with the maze-map so that it can sense, and infer how to 'close in' on, its quarry. This shows Cedric in a logical modality, in which it can eliminate movement possibilities in its enemy. In terms of the mazes A and B discussed earlier, this means ensuring that as it proceeds from start to finish it is certain that the enemy is not hiding in a blind alley. This presents the interesting problem for Cedric of going up a blind alley and then returning, after finding it empty, to wonder whether or not, while it was up there, its prey has slipped by towards the start.

The method of dealing with this situation is beyond Cedric and calls for Super-Cedric, unless you accept, as a human being would, the impossibility of being 'in two places at the same time'. If there were doors, it could lock them. It could possibly block the path to the start, but most likely its best method of approach would be to go up the blind alley and back as quickly as possible. But it can be seen now that Cedric must be able to accelerate and brake quickly and must be aware of when this is necessary. It is this last point that calls for the sort of reasoning which took us from Cedric to Super-Cedric, and seems best explained in terms of language.

Again, the point here is to notice that as in the case of ordinary applications of the Law of Effect, Cedric should feel pleasure in success and displeasure in failure. This is an assurance that it will survive by virtue of doing what is best for survival. Any other species, however Cedriclike in other respects, will not survive unless it has the property of doing the things necessary for survival.

So the pleasure and the pain are very much a part of the communication system. In fact, they are the major part of the internal communication system outside the brain and must also be represented inside the brain.

Some people have regarded the brain's main control activity as that of registering a misfit of some kind: hungry (this is a misfit, since food is missing) and look for food; thirsty and look for drink; and so on. This sort of process has been called a TOTE, where the letters TOTE stand for *T*est-*O*peration-*T*est-*E*xit. You test for a misfit, and if there is one you operate to fit it up; then you test again, and if it is now safe, you exit. You want to open a door: you try a key, and if it works, you unlock the door and go on to the next problem.

Such TOTES can interlock in a very complicated manner, and when they do, we call the processes involved 'thinking'. We have a misfit over hunger and then a misfit within the search for food over a map and another misfit on top of that over how to understand the map because some of it is missing, and we work back through the problem by first getting the missing map, putting it into the old map, next locating the food, and then consuming it. Such chains of activity are exactly the sort of complex maze-running type of activities we started with and now need to compound. TOTES within TOTES (so-called nested TOTES) are like choices within choices and are all essentially Boolean in form. The Boolean equivalent is something like the conditional state where we say A→B if and only if B→C, and B→C if and only if C→D, and so on (where → means 'implies'). As an algebraist you would probably use a symbol for 'if and only if' and if we choose ≡, as before, for that symbol, we have the sort of statement that makes our algebraist friends happy: $A \rightarrow B \equiv B \rightarrow C \cap B \rightarrow C \equiv C \rightarrow D$.

So it is that emotions in some form are necessary to any type of goal-seeking, and learning most certainly depends vitally upon goal-seeking. So emotions play a vital part in Super-Cedric and determine a large part of the internal information flow within Super-Cedric. Emotions are closely associated with motivations and there is no doubt that the internal drives and needs of human beings are strongly emotionally tinged. We have already made the point that this emotional colouring is necessary to survival because it allows the satisfaction of useful drives to be a source of pleasure and vice versa. The avoidance of unpleasant drives is a source of relief, which is a type of pleasure. The same points are valid for Super-Cedric. It can perform all its actions in a non-emotional way, but the most effective reinforcer to doing what is good and avoiding the bad is to associate the former with pleasure and the latter with pain.

I have already remarked that sex is one of the most important facets of behaviour when it comes to survival, and psychoanalysts have used sex as a basis for the explanation for most human behaviour. Although the urge for survival seems an adequate basis, it must be admitted that it is not the drive which sex is. Sex leads to copulation, hunger leads to eating, thirst leads to drinking, but survival leads to a much more diverse set of responses. It is clearly the source (or goal) of the pleasure-pain principle in all its aspects, and it is quite correct to link sex closely to survival. Perhaps, therefore, we should acknowledge the psychoanalysts' viewpoint and seek to explain much of human behaviour in terms of the underlying sexual motives.

If asked to explain behaviour, then it is natural to do so in terms of goals or motives. This immediately takes one to the drives and needs, which are basically instinctive and then are learned, by association, to apply to all other behaviour. So our motives are all linked to our instincts and it is these, with their close emotional associations, which are basic to all behaviour. As a result, we laugh and cry a lot and show emotion in almost everything we do.

The problem now for Super-Cedric is much the same. To be sure of survival we, as Super-Cedric's God, in effect, will make sure that the emotions are implanted as part of the communications net, since otherwise it may fail to survive.

The emotions, like all other systems, have spin-off; they do things they were not specifically designed to do. This is where creativity is involved and this is such an important aspect of the role of emotions that it merits a separate chapter.

What is important is that the emotions are less vital to Super-Cedric than they are to human beings, precisely because Super-Cedric does not need to go through the growing process which is essential to us, although of course it must, for survival, be capable of reproduction.

The most important point as far as human behaviour is concerned is that emotions and rational behaviour are completely integrated. Conative and cognitive behaviour are only completely distinguishable at the verbal level and should best be thought of as two aspects of the same thing, so that any explanations of human behaviour, and hence of Super-Cedric's behaviour, must be couched in terms of all aspects of that behaviour. We might just consider a single example of where emotions are important to Super-Cedric. It can hoot (as can Cedric) when things give pleasure, and the hoots can be varied, so that the listener can distinguish pleasure from pain and even different kinds of pleasure and different kinds of pain. We add to that an internal sensor, so that Super-Cedric is made to like some kinds of hoots and dislike others, or, more realistically, to like or dislike certain sets of inputs. This need only be specified in the basic design of Super-Cedric and then, by application of the process of secondary motivation, otherwise neutral features of the environment can cause pleasure and pain in their own right.

Lastly, we might consider some of the outward manifestations of emotion. When someone goes red or white in the face with anger or fear, we can as a result guess his state of mind. We say this is a sign of his internal state. Now this clearly is a spin-off. There is no sense in which such outward signs were intended by the designer of man – and that is presumably the evolutionary process – to demonstrate his internal states in this way; after all, the blood state which changes to facilitate action is only coincidentally visible in the facial state.

In a similar way, facial expressions and gestures are an outward sign of the workings of anyone's mind at a given time. Yet again, the natural set of people's faces gives some indication of their character. The heavily lined face, the sulky face (everyone knows the sort of range available) are all guides to behaviour and character.

Super-Cedric will not carry these external signs to any extent. It will be the ideal poker-player, or the Westerner's idea of the Oriental. Super-Cedric may display signs of emotion, of course, depending on its detailed design. If there were transparent covers on it we could possibly acquire, by the rate of the flashing of lights and their location, the same sort of information we can arrive at when Harry goes red with anger. But just as Harry goes red with anger, he could cover his face with a mask. The very fact that he does, of course, makes us suspicious about him, just as many people suspect the bearded person has something to hide.

Super-Cedric is automatically inscrutable, unless we as human beings design it to be otherwise. In fact, just as Super-Cedric will learn to stop us pulling out its plug when it becomes sufficiently intelligent, so it will learn to cover up its self-revealing parts. In much the same way, a human being wears dark glasses, although neither party can wholly cover its input systems, whether eyes or optical readers.

In the next chapter we examine the creative features of Super-Cedric, and their close involvement with emotions.

7 Creative Machines

Try imagining you're skimming on skis down
a very smooth slope. I used to play tennis
mentally when I was young and it often helped,
especially with new, very white balls.

Vladimir Nabakov, *Transparent Things*

What do we mean by 'creativity'? We mean formulating something new, solving some new problem or thinking some new thought. Creativity lies in the manner in which we deal with a situation not previously dealt with. It is clear that being creative can apply to a scientist or a technologist, an administrator, or indeed to anyone at all.

It is easy to overstate what is meant by creative ability. There seems to be nothing more involved than we have stated, and that places the main emphasis on the imaginative faculty. It is perfectly true that some people do have the most stimulating imagination and the results can include such things as relativity theory, nuclear energy, the sculpture of Epstein and the paintings of Rembrandt.

There is no suggestion being made here that these people – and many others too – are not creative geniuses, nor are we denying that it needs genius to attain their degree of creativity; all we are asking is what it is to be creative. We might guess that genius springs from having more of it (whatever *it* is) and perhaps also from having an almost fortuitous place and time in history, wherein such genius can manifest itself: having the right idea at the right time and knowing how to express it.

Now to Super-Cedric. Earlier it was described in a situation where it could communicate with other Super-Cedrics by describing its internal state to others in its community. But this is only helpful if the others know how to interpret its and their own internal states. In practice, with human beings, we communicate through language, gestures and expressions, and Super-Cedric found this also of great value whenever it wanted to communicate with others of its kind, always assuming they were not part of a sort of Siamese twin, sharing the same brain.

If now Super-Cedric wants to communicate emotions and feelings, as well as factual information, there will be a great deal to be said for its telling stories and painting pictures. It says, in effect, 'This is what I mean – like this', and it writes, paints, draws, etc. It may have a profound feeling about what it creates, since it feels its creation illustrates some very basic principle, as Einstein's theory of relativity yielded something profound about the nature of reality. There is an emotional overtone to the communication process whenever it occurs and the only question concerns, in any such situation, the ratio of emotion to reason.

It might be asked under what circumstances Super-Cedric would want to communicate its emotions and feelings, and the answer to this question provides a vital insight into our whole undertaking.

If Super-Cedric is to survive, it has to be able to do what is necessary for survival, similar to eating, drinking, or the machine equivalent in acquiring power. It also has to be a social being, since power for survival certainly can reside (up to a point) in numbers. If everything hinged on the survival of one particular human being, the hope for humanity would be almost nil. Now the need to communicate both satisfactions and dangers is part of the defensive cohesion of a society, and it is here that the need to communicate feelings and emotions arises.

The very existence of rhetoric in our society serves as a reminder that unless we create enormous emphasis by emotive means, then messages go unheeded. Furthermore, these messages do no more than highlight the extreme alarm state in a threatened system, and perhaps less obviously, but in the same way, the extreme satisfaction in rewards.

It is in this way that the feeling of emotions and the communication of that feeling is vital to a surviving species, and also lies at the basis of what we sometimes call creative art.

Some of the cognitive and conative aspects of Cedric, Super-Cedric and also of human beings, have already been described in some detail. We see them all now as social beings with language as the cement which binds society together – it may in some cases split it apart.

Our machine species of the future, and they will mostly be

Super-Cedrics (or Super-Super-Cedrics) are above all else social species which must be able, if they are to survive, to resist all threats from the external world. The resistance is perhaps most important when directed against inanimate threats – disease and so-called 'acts of God'. They will have to try to deal with them just as the human species deals with them.

In the same way they will have tried to grapple with and hoped to solve their own philosophical problems, their religious problems – should they arise – and their own creative problems. We shall look at each of these in turn.

Super-Cedric has the problem of deciding and understanding the nature of the world in which it was 'born'. It is the same problem for the human being. In the case of the human, he is born and acquires awareness by slow degrees, gradually appreciating more and more of the nature of his reality. He builds concepts, learns language, becomes familiar with his parents and starts his education in a sort of overlapping kaleidoscopic way. Super-Cedric has to cope with none of these problems, at least in nothing like the same way. We shall consider its quick birth and development.

Super-Cedric has all the storage space it wants (a potentially unlimited memory) and it has been constructed by a process of putting its parts together, as in a factory production process. It is eventually switched on, and starts to operate. We can in fact construct (or indeed another Super-Cedric can construct) it with its registers already in a fairly advanced state, which appears to give it 'instant consciousness'. This alone makes us ask whether or not our belief that consciousness is an inevitable property of highly complex 'intelligent systems' is justified. The answer to this is again yes, because it is impossible to have a highly intelligent system which is not self-referential. It must, as it uses language and has experience, be capable of inspecting itself and in so doing must realize that certain internally sensed states are in fact in existence within it.

If this is consciousness, then it cannot, of course, be instantaneous; it must rather depend upon each Super-Cedric discovering for itself the correlation between internal sensations and external stimuli. All one can say is that the process is likely to be extremely speedy; it will be much faster in Super-Cedric than in a child. It is perhaps a little like the awakening process after a human being has slept for quite a long period of time.

Super-Cedric then identifies the external world with its influence on itself, and thus appreciates that the external world is independent of itself. It realizes this because it can see that other things are touching other Super-Cedrics and it feels nothing, so it concludes quite correctly that they are not touching it. Quite quickly then it formulates the idea that real people, independent of itself, inhabit the world.

It may well never consider the more subjective forms of philosophy because it does not mature through that period where outside things are shadowy and difficult to distinguish from each other, or from itself.

Super-Cedric can 'read' philosophy, so it knows what (other) philosophers have said; therefore it acquires the idea, for example, of the subjective and the objective. In saying that Super-Cedric can read, I mean that it can take in and digest all the recorded statements of mankind. Whether this is done by literally reading books, or by processing books into tapes – a community activity – and then feeding on the tapes, is in a sense a minor administrative decision which will, in the end, be determined by the way in which we as human beings develop Super-Cedric and the way it subsequently decides to evolve itself when it is emancipated.

But my aim is not to write a treatise on philosophy, merely to note in rather general terms how Super-Cedric will build up its own view of the world. In what way will this view differ from a human's view? The answer seems to be that it might not differ at all, but we have to stand back now and remember to say that since Super-Cedric will ultimately be so much more intelligent than we are, we can only guess at its conclusions. In much the same way a man from the fourteenth century would only be able to guess at Bertrand Russell's conclusions: are they, though, so very different as conscious entities?

If philosophy is independent of science, Super-Cedric's view will not be so different from our own, but I personally will hazard the guess that it will develop a rationalistic empiricist view of reality and perhaps in its social life become reasonably pragmatic, so that its empiricism and pragmatism will become very different from our own, in the detail if not in the broad sweep. If, though, science does radically change philosophy or even significantly influence it, then we cannot anticipate the dizzy possibilities that lie ahead.

The interrelatedness of philosophy and science deserves a brief mention, although it could easily fill a whole series of volumes. Many philosophers believe they are dealing with eternal truths that have always been, and always will be, truths. Other philosophers believe that their views are coloured by what we discover as scientists about the nature of reality. This crude distinction will serve to make clear that opinions on whether or not Super-Cedric's philosophy will be much as ours, or vastly different, will hinge on which view one has of philosophy.

Super-Cedric's philosophical problems can clearly take various forms. Suppose that it sees life as a transaction between itself and other species, and an environment in which it has evolved: its theory of evolution will not be quite the same as the current Darwin-based theory widely accepted by human beings, because it will believe in offspring-manufacture as a natural process, rather than the way we think of reproduction as natural. In other words it will see that the evolutionary process is something in the hands of people and machines, and a matter for them to decide. It is for humans to say what should be the next stage of development, and not 'nature' or 'God'. In other words, evolution may appear more a 'mental' and less a physical thing to Super-Cedric, as soon as it realizes that it was itself a product of man's imagination.

Next comes the question of religion. Following our usual tactic of asking how human beings behave, we might ask how human beings came to believe in God. The answer now is more equivocal than the answers to other questions which have arisen in our search for the means of synthesizing intelligent behaviour. What it amounts to is that some people would presumably argue that it was a matter of being aware that a God existed; and others, at the other extreme, would argue that we naively invented God to answer the sort of questions we could not answer ourselves, and to deal with the sort of problems we could not deal with ourselves. This latter view was certainly held by Freud, who thought that belief in God was belief in an illusion.

Our automaton, I believe, would come down on the Freudian side of the fence and would also form the belief that the world was a kind of 'scientific' accident. But once more we have to admit to being unable to anticipate the dizzy possibilities that lie in the future for Super-Cedric and its species.

In the light of these comments on a sort of machine rationalism, it is worth asking ourselves about the machine's artistically, creative ability. Under what circumstances could, or would, works of art be created and what would they mean?

Thinking back to the origin of language as being partly pictorial and partly acoustic, we can think of people as drawing and painting pictures on the one hand, and making noises on the other. The noises referred primarily to the sort of pictures which people frequently saw. Then it must have been obvious that some people made sounds, and created drawings and paintings, better than others. This in turn led to the emergence of the tribal artists and scribes.

Variations in techniques in both these activities would certainly lead to some people developing altogether new forms. This would lead to poetry and blank verse on the one hand, and to different types of drawings, varying from the realistic to the symbolic, on the other, and performed in all sorts of different media.

This is no place to discuss a theory of the history of art and literature, any more than philosophy, but from these simple beginnings, urged on by emotions which derived pleasure, and by implication also some pain, from their efforts, human beings acquired the origin of the arts.

That the emotions play a major part in these artistic activities is undoubted. In the same way as the pleasure-pain principle operates to give satisfaction on being fed when hungry, so a good picture or a good piece of prose gives satisfaction when seen or read. It is more than this, in so far as either the recall or the recognition of pleasant events will give pleasure. A story then becomes a well-written account of some events either experienced or imagined. We should pause over the word 'imagined'.

When we imagine something, we do one of two things. We either construct an event not personally experienced, or construct an event never experienced by any person at all. The process is always basically one of constructing events out of concepts. It is very much along the lines described earlier. Something new to us can only be described in terms which are already familiar. So when we imagine, we construct the unknown or unknowable in terms which are familiar. A man is familiar, a house is familiar, blue is familiar, and so on. We can now imagine a blue man in a blue house. It is clear that the mechanism involved in imagination is independent of whether or not the scene imagined has actually occurred.

So, returning to literature, we tell stories which refer to people imagined, in either of the two senses in which we have used that word; they are necessarily, even if about real people, partly imagined, since it is impossible to know all the detail about those people. It is because no one fits exactly into the story you want to tell, that you have to invent characters who do. But why tell a story at all? The reason is partly for teaching purposes. We teach by example, and if necessary invent the story to suit our purposes. It is also to inform in simple terms, so that a point can be illustrated without using an actual historical example.

The story tells the reader, perhaps, something we want him to believe about reality. It tells us that people can be human and kind, and generous even in adversity. It tells us that love can surmount most hurdles. Perhaps the parables told by Jesus sufficiently illustrate the point.

We can now add all the ingredients that the history of literature – both prose and poetry – well illustrates. But there is another side to it. The whole gamut of human activities which earmark man as irrational, prejudiced, and otherwise unstable or unreasonable, are in some way connected with the emotions. Sometimes it is entirely a matter of supporting a viewpoint which is known by the owner of the view to be quite wrong, but is nevertheless a cherished view. In other cases it involves the determination to believe certain things irrespective of the evidence. It could be that this is man's state in believing much of what he believes. His religious convictions, for example, probably quite often misnamed as 'convictions', are illustrative of a point where just such a state of affairs might apply.

Even Super-Cedric 1, though, can be made to perform some creative activity. If wishing to communicate its feelings to

Super-Cedric 2, on having caught its prey, it could use its hooter, not just to sound off once, but in effect to play a tune. There is a precedence for this sort of thing even in early computing, where a hooter was sometimes attached to the control and the tune which followed was indicative of the state of the machine; perhaps here lie the beginnings of computer music.

It should be said that there is in existence a great deal of art, music, poetry and the like, constructed by a computer. We would on balance regard this as falling foul of Lady Lovelace's well-known objection that 'the computer only does what it is made to do'. In other words, such artistic creations are really those of the programmer. To be genuine, computer art must occur in systems such as Super-Cedric in which the *need* to create art is felt because of the accompanying emotions and the desire to communicate.

The evocation of memories, the awareness of tragedy, the feeling of almost infinite beauty, the sense of love . . . all these things form the conceptual bases of artistic creation. We could go on at length to try, however inadequately, to capture the spirit of art at its best. Magic can occur in words:

But look, the morn, in russet mantle clad,
Walks o'er the dew of yon high eastern hill.

This is a far cry from the revelation of one's store contents. Or is it? The intervening gap is covered by genius, and that is not impossible to reproduce in Super-Cedric. But just as Japanese music seems remote to a Western ear, so the genius of the literary machine will, in all probability, be lost on the mind of the human being.

The best hope, though, perhaps lies in 'love'. If the emotional system in Super-Cedric is strong enough, then the result must be a literature as profound as that created by human beings, even if more remote to us than the writings of Gertrude Stein. The question which will constantly recur is the price to be paid for this emotionalism and its creative aspect.

Finally we should be clear that art is social. It stems from the need to communicate with others, and like all communication it is born of living in a society with others, and wanting to share feelings and experience. Language and communication is also a vital cement which binds society together and hopefully gives some unity of purpose.

In primitive society, the unity of purpose was a basic tool of survival. As society becomes more complex, as in the western world at the end of the twentieth century, that purpose can become diffuse and it could be so diffuse as to destroy society itself. It seems that the machine species which may inherit the earth will be burdened by the same social problems, and consoled by the same artistic creations, as human beings are.

8 Automation and Cybernation

In recent years the effects and advances in information technology on society have been viewed as more disruptive than any previous technological impact.

John McHale, *The Changing Information Environment*

The new machine species has so far been discussed by way of the use of the models Cedric and Super-Cedric, and I have dealt extensively with the input and processing of both cognitive and conative information. We need also to consider output. Much output activity is fairly obvious, as in the case of the movement of Cedric in its maze-running. A great deal more is also obvious in the case of Super-Cedric, in its utterance of language and its use of gestures in communication. But certain aspects of output are embodied in the field of automation. We could indeed say that it is automation that has directly led to the emergence of the Cedrics in the first place.

We have in part, in this chapter, to indulge in a sort of flash-back to an earlier stage of development. This is necessary because much that occurs under the name of automation became a reality prior to the general realization of the possibility of a machine species, and is therefore well-known, or certainly better known than the rest of our story. It is nevertheless necessary to recapitulate some of what is entailed and by that means work up to the present and future.

As in the case of our arguments so far, such as the use of cameras for eyes and radios for ears, so we can look to automation for relatively simple control systems. It then ranges over all sorts of more complicated possibilities.

The reason automation preceded cybernetics is that it was easier to amplify muscle power and leave it under human brain control, than vice versa. Furthermore, it was thought by many that brain amplification was an impossibility: there was something magic about mentality that was difficult, even in principle impossible, to stimulate, or even synthesize. This we no longer believe.

Automation is, or at least can be thought of as, *applied cybernetics*. This is perhaps not historically accurate, since automation really came first in the form of self-controlling factories, and in the engineering of automatic control systems. But now that the theory has overtaken the practice, we can think of automation as being the application of cybernetic ideas, ranging from single feedback controls to very complicated ones like Super-Cedric.

Automation is concerned with the automatic control of machinery. Once upon a time men and women performed all such everyday control tasks as stamping forms, cashing cheques, issuing payrolls, writing up the ledger. Now they can all be done and many are being done, by machines, and mostly, in various forms, by the computer: both special-purpose and general-purpose, digital and analogue, but mostly the former.

We should first consider a well-known early example of automation – the automatic pilot 'George'. Many human pilots have used it and most people have heard of it. But we should look to see how it works.

The principles involved in George are exceptionally simple. An aircraft is controlled as to its direction of flight by its rudder, elevators and ailerons. We set the desired positions for each, and then if they are displaced from the desired position by bumpiness or whatever, we record the fact, thus changing the direction of flight. The human pilot registers the fact visually by watching his instruments and, where possible, by noting that the aircraft has changed its position with respect to the horizon. All we need, in order to replace the pilot for the purpose of keeping the aircraft on course, is a sensitive element that records the error in position and immediately provides the equivalent compensation on the control. It is like driving a car; if you see that you are too far to the left you rotate your steering wheel to the right.

To build such a device once provided quite a problem for engineers, but they mastered it. They began then to understand the principle of control through what was called *negative feedback*. This is the process of being provided with the information which makes you correct any error by a correction operating in the opposite direction, a matter I have mentioned in the context of 'knowledge of results'. This is a very powerful method and applies to hosts of different systems such as the human brain and other internal body organs. To maintain purposes and achieve goals, you must know the results of your action. This is where we have referred to TOTES in our previous discussion. In modern terms the subject is called control engineering.

George, the automatic pilot, was used to keep a steady direction and steady speed of flight. Bumpiness in the air made control movements necessary and these control (i.e. correcting) movements could be made automatically. But the human pilot was still there to make sure that all went well. George was never intended to be a substitute pilot, although it could do a part of the pilot's job very well indeed.

The social effects of automation have been simple and straightforward, on the whole. The economic facts of life limit the extent to which we can build motorways and freeways, however desirable they may be; similarly, the progress of automatic controls will be relatively slow. We may well replace the least skilled of human beings first, since the simplest operations are usually the easiest to automate. All activities can be automated, but not all at once. We have to consider economic factors. In the long run it is obvious that men are more costly than machines, and as a result machines are inevitably to be used more and more to replace men. This is particularly the case as the machines become more and more efficient. Nor need their cost go up significantly, since machines can manufacture themselves. Most commentators on automation tacitly assume that machine costs will rise proportionately to human labour costs, since human beings are needed to make machines. But this is not true. The most urgently needed machines are those for making machines, where *both* machines – those that do the making *and* those made – are automatic and self-controlling. This is one of the many ways in which cybernetics changes altogether our picture of the future automated society. It is also interesting to see the obvious relationship which exists between industrial production and biological reproduction. Machines can, as I shall show, reproduce themselves, as well as repair and maintain themselves. This does not necessarily mean that overnight the influx of such machines, which will transform our society, will occur; if such a thing did happen, it would precipitate a world crisis, and could lead to the destruction of the human race. But it does mean the gradual emergence of such machines which, taken together with cybernetic machines, imply the emergence of our new machine species. As time goes by we are more and more inclined to omit the word 'gradual'. The growth and implied social changes are in fact exponential.

Before we leave this important economic matter, it must be said again that although economics is obviously a matter of great importance in all scientific and technological development, there is no reason to believe that it will provide any barrier to our man-machine development. One other development which has already taken place is that of automated flying, and it has made a jumbo jet into an aircraft that could be virtually regarded as a specialized Super-Cedric.

It should be noted here that this comes very near to an example of a machine – in the traditional sense – which was originally intended to be completely controlled by a human being becoming almost completely controlled by a 'computer' ('machine' in our sense of the term). We shall take a closer look at the jumbo jet.

The modern jumbo jet has an automatic take-off control, an automatic landing system, and an automatic flying control system together with an automatic navigational system. This is such a powerful set of automatic procedures that one jumbo jet pilot has said: 'All I have to do is taxi the aircraft out to take-off, and when I arrive in New York, select the amount of brake I need to touch down and taxi the aircraft into the hangar.' He felt that by the time these words were read, even that amount of manual interference would almost certainly be a thing of the past. This is rather like Cedric becoming Super-Cedric, or George becoming Super-George.

The navigational system is of special interest to us. It takes over on the ground (in London, say) when its position is established. About fifteen minutes are needed by the computer to absorb this information and then the aircraft takes off and is landed in New York. If the navigational system was ten miles out in pinpointing New York, it would be regarded as a very bad piece of handiwork. But the most interesting aspect of the system is that when it has been told that 'this is New York' while it thinks it is ten miles west of New York, then again having absorbed the facts, it reconstructs its trip and learns some part, or all, of where the error occurred. You can be sure that next time we shall arrive at New York and not ten miles away. *It learns from experience* and learns by systematically going through all the events of the trip after it is completed. It is very much like a person, who, having carried out a lengthy and complex task, goes away and thinks about it all and inspects his records of what happened and is enjoined 'to do better next time': the very epitome of good learning.

We should notice another point. If you have a situation in which men and machines cooperate, then sooner or later the machine is almost certain to take over. In decision-taking, the situation leads to the 'Civil Service Syndrome' where the man cannot afford to take the risk of disagreeing with the computer. If the man is correct he gains little, but if he is wrong he stands to lose everything. Much of the time, even the pilot is in the hands of his automatic controls: he disputes them at his risk, and therefore does so very rarely.

In automatic landings in fog, for example, there is no way he dares to take over ('pull out the plug' on the machine) himself, since the machine can be shown to be almost always right. This same point was well-known to human pilots of the earliest days of flying blind in cloud. They had to trust their instruments and never their senses: if they did the latter, they nearly always finished up dead.

I would like next to place automation in the context of Super-Cedric's activities. We started with Cedric and moved to Super-Cedric to cater for increased brainpower. There was then seen to be no reason for following – at least in the short term – the 'biological accidents' of nature in keeping our new expanding brain moving around, so Super-Cedric could, as a result, acquire any number of detached 'limbs'.

The 'limbs' we had in mind for Super-Cedric were Cedric, or a whole set of 'fags' like Cedric, moving limbs and anything else which might be a convenience for Super-Cedric. The fact is that Super-Cedric can select from the whole range of mechanization and automation. The automated equipment is especially convenient because it is already self-controlling equipment and

Super-Cedric's overriding control is made that much easier. Automation is to Super-Cedric what labour-saving devices are to the twentieth-century housewife: a must!

Automation and its development provided in fact the beginnings of the Second Industrial Revolution and cybernation is carrying through to its natural conclusion: the Third Industrial Revolution.

It will not be difficult to see that the emergence of Super-Cedric involves a 'takeover' of all that has been briefly outlined in this chapter: automated domestic life, automated transport, automated organization of every kind. The Super-Cedrics could take this one step forward and we as humans could become a subjugated people, living in a 'cybernated world' controlled by an artificial species of our own making.

To take one further, but temporary, step back and consider again the matter of control systems in a quasi-historical context: it is worth reflecting for a moment on the degree of control we as human beings are likely to be able to exercise on machines as they become increasingly sophisticated. We find it easy enough to control the obviously docile machines such as a bicycle, although cars and aircraft provide problems: they are less docile. Simple negative-feedback systems are rather more difficult (Cedrics) but we can always 'pull out the plug' on them, and we should ask ourselves under what conditions we could no longer 'pull out the plug' of 'more intelligent machines': all this we have discussed and we know that the point can quickly be reached where we cannot 'pull out the plug' (Super-Cedrics). Suppose we decide to build individual machines to wage war for us. We would need to make them highly flexible, since they are *not* going to have a human controller, and without great flexibility they would be an easy prey to an enemy. What we have to do is build a great deal of humanlike intelligence into the machine, and it is worth thinking carefully how this should be done; we are, in effect, building a robot soldier: another specialized Cedric, or Super-Cedric.

We should notice that we have a hierarchy of systems ranging from sub-sub-Cedric (e.g. pickaxes), through sub-Cedric (which can, however, be used for making Cedric), Cedric and Super-Cedric. Sub-Cedric and sub-sub-Cedrics are used in the manufacture of the whole family. It is a little like the human progression, where one starts with uncontrolled action, then self-controlled action, learning and then learning to learn.

It must also be remembered that in building intelligent machines we are directly copying human beings. It is essential to see the purposive and goal-seeking nature of our problem. The measure of success of any action is the extent to which its goal is achieved. By this means of assessing the 'degree of success', a human being or an 'intelligent machine' can modify the behaviour needed for the future (feedback again). We ourselves achieve the flexibility which characterizes human behaviour partly by the dangerous business of associations with success or failure, likes and dislikes (secondary motivation again). We need such flexibility in our autonomous 'machine soldier', and there can be no guarantee that it, with its newly designed independence, so necessary for its job, will not turn against its makers.

The situation is, in some ways, absurd, yet quite real. One sees perhaps a glimmer of hope from the way we have controlled actual human beings in the past. After all, they have not always rebelled against authority and turned on their makers. But here there are problems, since human beings have a 'conscience' (the result of moral instruction) and have emotions which are dragooned by early training.

Music, poetry and religion tend to work towards harmony, and provide a sense of satisfaction in humans which compensates for much of the drudgery they have to suffer; and all this, as was suggested in the previous chapter, will be true of Super-Cedric. The snag is that our machine will have no such emotions, unless we take the (necessary) risk of building them in. It will anyway be motivated to eliminate an enemy, but will also have the flexibility and 'intelligence' to modify motivations through experience. We have to be sure that the modifications enacted will not lead to the elimination of ourselves. Such an assurance cannot be forthcoming beyond a certain level of intelligence and emotion in the machine; and this is how we could therefore make a new species which is more efficient than we are ourselves. We would not have to give this species the power to reproduce itself. If we give it the intelligence and the ability to learn, it will discover for itself how to reproduce itself. It may run into a shortage of raw materials, but so has the human race, and Super-Cedrics will be more likely to find the answer than we will – probably by synthetic means.

On the domestic scene, automatically controlled cars, as well as aircraft, are clearly possible and, as a result, the car driver can be released to carry out other activities while he is being conveyed from place to place. These will involve local journeys only, since for longer journeys monorail trains, and aircraft, are inevitable – with or without car-ferry facilities.

Our domestic life will clearly be wholly automated and nowhere more obviously so than in the home itself. Consider the kitchen. We can automate this quite easily. The input into our automated cooking system is the raw material – the groceries we buy, and the meats and poultry, bread, milk, etc, we keep in the larder. Much of this can be circulated by other means than those used effectively by the present supermarket methods, but at the moment we shall not concentrate on this aspect of the problem, but assume that the raw materials are both needed and available.

The next stage can be completely automated, even down to the choice of meals, since an automated 'market research' system can be built into the 'kitchen' and food will be supplied in the knowledge of market prices and availability conjoined to known preferences in foodstuffs.

The next phase which may well have been reached by the year 2000 is that of taking food in the form of pills. But psychological needs rather than nutritional needs will probably still provide at least one meal per day. Many may consider this to be nonsense; but there is ample evidence of the possibility, in purely scientific terms.

The process of 'rethinking' was described earlier; this is a vital process in many phases of life and it is important to grasp the principle clearly. It was mentioned in the context of George, the automatic pilot, but I shall repeat it. In building the automatic control systems, we would be stupid to try to manufacture artificial 'eyes' to read the various dials showing height, airspeed and the like that are currently standard input equipment in an aircraft cockpit. Visual displays in the form of dials are purely for human eyes. If we do not have human controls, we do not *need* visual displays. This means that the automatic pilot of tomorrow can receive details of airspeed communicated directly into its control system. Because of such rethinking, huge simplifications must be achieved. This principle affects all automated developments (remember the principle of *synthesis*).

To look very briefly now at electronics: the most important current landmark is the development of the microprocessor. The transistor and integrated circuits are already water under the bridge, but the microprocessor is only just beginning to show its mettle. As a typical example, a single microprocessor can be programmed to simultaneously monitor and control a set of petrol pumps, keeping track of the amount of petrol delivered by each pump and calculating all the accounts that are linked to it. It is also microprocessors which make Cedric and Super-Cedric possible at the small size – or relatively small size – they are.

The home computer which can deal with our domestic life is already approaching reality, thanks to microprocessors. The computer will be a microprocessor which will be linked to the television, the telephone and a small keyboard. The facilities that such a system could provide are virtually without limit, but the most obvious examples are security control, entertainment, shopping, data retrieval and control of the domestic environment. The microprocessor will act as a security system and will monitor door and window sensors to detect intruders. Heat and gas sensors will detect fire and warn of gas leaks. An alarm will automatically be sounded if burglars, fire or leaking gas are detected, and will also call the police or the fire brigade by telephone. The television screen can be used to show a plan of the house on which the location of the burglar or the fire can be pinpointed.

Home computers of the kind I have described have several obvious benefits to offer. Housebreaking would become a much more hazardous occupation; and as an added deterrent, the house owner would be able to program the computer to turn lights on and off when the house was empty. Elderly people would be able to maintain stronger contact with the outside world, and if they lived on their own they would have the security of knowing that if, for example, they hurt themselves or fell and could not move, the computer would automatically summon assistance. The social implications of such controls are not necessarily in every way good for people. This is fairly obvious and we can see the dangers of laziness and boredom looming up here.

Microprocessors will play a prominent part in all forms of transport. On the railways they are already used for signalling-equipment inside the driving-cab. This enables train drivers to be warned of any dangers along the line. Because rail traffic follows a predetermined timetable, it is easy to let thousands of microprocessors take over part – or even the whole – of the running of the system.

Road traffic is less predictable, but even so, microprocessors will be used to reduce traffic jams, prevent dangerous driving and locate missing and stolen cars. Microprocessors will be used in two ways in this area: as part of the traffic control system and as a unit inside every car. A small number of cars incorporate microprocessors already, but computers inside them may be a standard feature in a few years' time. At first microprocessors will be used to control the car's engine, allowing a very accurate control of ignition leading to reduced pollution, greater mileage and overall better performance. Microprocessors may be used inside cars in an entirely different way, as navigational and locative aids. By picking up signals from wires buried underneath the road surfaces, the microprocessor in the car will be able to communicate with a control computer located in a local traffic control centre. Each car would then be able to respond to or transmit a unique identifying code. The central computer would be able to send instructions to the individual car and the microprocessor in the car would interpret these instructions and inform the driver – whether human or computer.

A driver who was unfamiliar with the roads of a large city, such as New York, would be able to tell the central computer where he wanted to go and would then be told which way to go at every road junction. The central computer would be able to separate local traffic from through traffic, the driver would be instructed to follow routes which avoided crowded roads, and all traffic would be automatically diverted away from the scenes of accidents.

Another way in which microprocessors could be used in cars,

apart of course from driving them, is to detect and prevent dangerous driving, whether due to alcohol, fatigue, or whatever. By monitoring the speed of cars, their acceleration and steering parameters and their distance from other vehicles, the microprocessor would be able to decide whether or not the car was being properly driven. Signals from the buried wires would inform the microprocessor of the appropriate speed limit. If the microprocessor found that the car was being improperly driven, it would be able to alert the driver, inform the police via the central computer or even automatically pull over and stop the car. Drivers who wandered on to the wrong side of the road, drove too close to the car in front or overtook at dangerous points would therefore be known immediately, and would not be able to escape detection.

Unfortunately, like all inventions that *can* benefit the human race, microprocessors can be put to less welcome uses. Chief among these is surveillance and all that the data-bank society implies. I must say a little about this highly important by-product of automation.

Access control, i.e. allowing access to buildings or parts of buildings only to individuals presenting valid cards, is already an important part of the security arrangements for important establishments such as power stations, military camps and research centres. With the availability of cheap microprocessors, this concept can be applied almost everywhere: in hospitals, libraries, stations, banks and airports. An identity card bearing a secret code number can be used and then we would only need card-readers at the entrance to public buildings, buses, trains, etc to complete the trick. This does have some benefits in making travel, for example, much simpler. There would be no need to buy tickets for train journeys, since it would be simple for the microprocessor in the train's card-reader to check the credit-rating for the card presented to it.

A single identity card would thus take the place of all the credit cards, driving-licences, library tickets, etc we carry around, and eventually it may even replace cash. The more sinister implication here is that the police would be able to track the movements of any individual: it would be extremely difficult to obtain medical treatment, draw money from a bank, board a train or drive a car without the police being notified of the exact time and place of the event.

It is impossible at this stage to predict the overall effect the microprocessor will have on our daily lives by the mid-1980s, because so much depends on the political and social climates in which the technology develops. Much of the frustration of contemporary urban life could be eliminated; no one need spend time doing dull routine jobs, and the crime rate could be sharply cut. All these things are possible, but it is equally possible (almost certain, indeed) that we may find ourselves living in a totalitarian world.

We may, in fact, in the light of all these changes, alter our community life in the future and move away from individual private houses to something more like interrelated networks of motels; this suggests community life with a difference, not necessarily totalitarian. In turn it suggests the emergence of new linear cities which are built around motorways, stretching across whole continents, from New York to Los Angeles and from Perth to Sydney.

There are many difficulties involved in replanning and reorganizing the process of living in society, as the very act of replanning is itself part of living in that society; we cannot 'stop the world and get off'. We can never get wholly outside ourselves, either as individuals or as groups. We are never privileged observers, outside the system of things, so all we do must be done implicitly. The principle of implicitness applies everywhere. If we wish to reconstruct or reorganize a factory and change our form of production, or if we wish to incorporate new designs into various arts and crafts, such as architecture or town planning, or the building of new highways, then we have to face the difficulty of changeover, the transition from one state to another. The evolution must come from within. It is a reminder of Dr Otto Neurath's comment on philosophy: 'It is like completely rebuilding a ship while still at sea.'

We are always in a state of transition, and still we have not become fully aware that transitions are our *normal* process of evolution, not by any means the abnormal times that they are sometimes thought to be. This is another way of saying that society has been slow to recognize the vitally important nature of change, and this I have already extensively emphasized. It still remains a fact, of course, that some periods of change are faster than others, and the tendency is to change faster all the time. Many of these things have been brought into focus by cybernetics and automation.

We have to remember too, that most human beings are not used efficiently by the community in our present society. The bulk of jobs are automatic and require no insight, and yet they are performed by human beings and the result is chronic boredom. Human beings are being used to imitate machines, and nowhere is this more obvious than in the armed services. Should our educational system do what we ask of it, we shall have better educated people in our community. If such people are not released from such dull routine jobs, we simply sow the seeds of discontent, rising to the point of violence and revolution. The difficulty is the real transition period between ignorance and education, and this could be fatal to civilization.

Since we know that people are only happy when they have something to complain about, there can be no suggestion that people will be any happier living in the automated world of the twenty-first century, if we ever get that far. Happiness is something to do with the ratio of ambition to achievement, as well as one's physiological state, and has little or nothing to do with the material standards of the time. People are happy when they are physically fit and physiologically efficient, provided they have a fair measure of success in life, and no obvious weakness which they let become an obsession. They also need to have complaints (even if a minimum of complaints) at all times. This again in Super-Cedric shows the need for internal awareness both of the state of its automatic working mechanisms and of its brain, and raises the whole matter of the motivation and purpose which would act as a drive for the Super-Cedric society; this forms an important part of my next chapter. For the remainder of this chapter, though, we shall look at the short-term threat to human liberty of existing automation.

This threat is easily seen to be connected with the use of microprocessors, which will assist in allowing and maintaining every type of surveillance and make way for the Super-Cedric society which will then make the contents of this chapter less significant: by then the damage will be complete, although it should be made clear that the 'data-bank' society is something already with us and will, unless we learn to control it, destroy us before Super-Cedric arrives. It is ironic that the destruction is already with us at the sub-Cedric level of activities, thanks to huge and fast memory stores and their abuse by society.

The current problems stem from the huge increase in capacity of existing processing systems and the great decrease in their cost. To look first at a quote from Donald Madgwick:

> The Precision Instrument Company of Palo Alto, California, demonstrated the model of a new laser process capable of putting 645 million bits of data on one square inch of tape.

Donald Madgwick goes on to say even more dramatic things on the subject:

> Photocromic micro-images have made it possible for the complete Bible to be reproduced on a thin sheet of plastic less than two inches square. Furthermore, a single unit of any one 4,800-foot reel of one-inch plastic tape, using the laser memory process, will be capable of storing in digital form up to twenty pages of information for every man, woman and child in the USA, and one should note that that means roughly 5,000 words can be put into a dossier for every man, woman and child in the USA.

More recently McHale has quoted:

> ... within two years, existing technology would enable us to keep track of the important facts about everyone in the world, at a cost of five cents each. Furthermore, this information would, for all practical purposes, be available instantly.

We can multiply examples of this same thinking many times over, but the name of Professor Westin should at least be mentioned. He points out (as Nigel Calder and others have) how huge investigative systems, both private and governmental, have arisen for the purpose of control and surveillance of the community.

Next we shall briefly concentrate our attention on the manner in which complex computer networks could be used, say, by the *police force* in a country such as Britain. We must assert straight away that we are not attempting to describe the actual police network in Britain. Most inquirers into such police computer units are told that the acquisition of such information could offend against the Official Secrets Act!

In Chicago, for example, there is a police detection system which is surprisingly insensitive to the need for the safeguarding of privacy. It is apparently used to inform the city's education authorities of juvenile delinquency! In most Western countries, though, we now have a police computer network which stores fingerprints as well as the normal information about people. This is in line with police procedure, but once more by virtue of the vast size and speeds of data banks, the quantitative change becomes a qualitative one, as in the case of the change from ordinary to nuclear bombs. The trouble is that efforts move from detecting crime to anticipating it, which steps up the surveillance of the individual, and quickly erodes all privacy. Such lists of people kept on file need not be restricted to those with criminal records, since there seems no legal obligation to exclude any number of others, who, for example, might be regarded as suspects or be thought of as associates of criminals.

If a crime is committed, the details can be entered in exactly the same way as a program can be run or updated on a teletypewriter. We now have the obvious search for those who are usually concerned with such crimes, where they were last seen and whether they are in prison, and so on. This involves using means which are really approximate statistical correlations of the type we frequently meet in market research. We come up with a list of suspects who are identified as wanted for questioning. In certain circumstances where information is much more specific, say in the case of identified fingerprints, the search is then for the single suspect. We must remember that the whole operation of searching data files, including looking for statistical correlations, is done at astronomical speeds, characteristic, as we know, of the computer.

The fact that computer codes can easily be broken is something of which I have had direct experience. There has been much breaking of codes by students, even at the Massachusetts Institute of Technology's vast experimental project MAC

(Machine Aided Cognition), in spite of the elaborate precautions taken to ensure privacy. This is by no means an isolated example.

Professor Miller says:

> Computer experts at the University of Michigan . . . tell me that a programmer with less than a month's training can break the most elaborate procedures currently being used in large data banks . . . within five hours.

It appears that at the University of Michigan the authorities purposely leave a terminal unattended. Students, specifically encouraged to try, have never yet failed to break the access code and get into the system. Naturally, the personnel servicing the central processor is another weak link in the security chain. Professor Miller again says:

> The programmer, for instance, could insert a secret 'door' in the monitor program that would enable unauthorized people to bypass protective devices, or could 'bug' a machine in such a sophisticated manner that it might remain unnoticed for an extensive period.

Then there is the problem of wiretapping, which applies when computerized data leave the central processor for the peripherals. There are innumerable ways in which this could be done. To mention just a few:

1. Planting a 'door' in the control program.
2. Bugging the transmission line.
3. Cancelling a user's sign-off signal and continuing the system under the user's name.

Now we come to the switching centre and the remote console. Again there are various weaknesses involved, but two stand out. They are the accidental or intentional making of wrong corrections, and the cracking of the relevant codes.

It is obvious that computer records are easier to destroy than ordinary paper files. Some incidents have already been recorded – and many more have occurred – whereby information on magnetic tapes was completely destroyed. Professor Miller quotes a case where a disgruntled employee virtually destroyed his employer's complete business records: all too easy a thing to do.

I shall not attempt a complete documentation of the weaknesses of computer nets as data banks. It is clear that, on technical grounds alone, a computer network is something which is easily defiled, and we have to think of the consequences of such weaknesses in the light of huge data banks set up by the police, the armed services, insurance companies, prisons, debt collectors, medical institutions, and the like. There are two dangers which are obvious, and they could become the same one. If they were integrated across a country or a continent or even ultimately across the entire world, then the threat to individual liberty would be altogether obvious, if only because of the very efficiency with which information about us would be available. If, on the other hand, such various data-bank networks were kept separate, any one investigator – for example, a blackmailer or other type of criminal – could fairly easily acquire information from the nets and provide his own integrated picture. If, of course, the information was already integrated, much of the hard work would have been done for him, and he would only have to break through one security code.

Looking at the matter from another point of view, we have to recognize the importance of the actual information pollution which can occur in such data-file situations, even when wholly good intentions are present. It is quite clear that the centralization of information can lead to distortion. Information, as we know from studies in logic and semantics, is to some extent contextually defined, and as information from a large number of different sources is linked together, so it can be that distortion occurs.

The image of infallibility associated with computers lends credence to data banks and manifestly increases their effectiveness and thus their dangers. Of course, there are innumerable stories describing computer inefficiency, but most people realize quite correctly that the computer is not usually at fault, rather it is those who use the computer. The difficulties with the interpretation of information on data files are entirely concerned with human beings and their methods of interpretation.

Some people believe they know what is best for others;

democracy, as a result, is always in a tenuous and potentially unstable state. In their fight against opposition – whether criminal, trade union or merely political – governments will gradually be tempted beyond endurance and will start to exercise their powers. The data-bank society, in conjunction with all the other scientific techniques of control, will help to make totalitarianism inevitable. Finally, then, we shall look at what might be done by judicial means to avoid the consequences of our data-banks, but even if we avoid such totalitarianism, we still have to avoid the consequences of the machine species and its threat of takeover.

It seems that we need a framework of law in which to exercise the necessary restraints to prevent the misuse of power with respect to information pollution. Some clarificatory work must be carried out on the definitions of privacy, and limits must be established as to how far we should be prepared to have our existing privacy further invaded in the interests of organizational efficiency.

The setting-up of new organizations – as well as the use of existing organizations – is also required. These organizations must try to establish full awareness of the problems and in particular to establish standards of acceptable behaviour with respect to the use of personal information. An attempt must clearly be made to preserve freedom without destroying all efficiency.

Law groups, scientists and business people must at the very least be involved in these efforts and must therefore themselves first be fully appraised of the facts. We must understand existing methods of record-keeping and must be clear as to how these are likely to be changed by computerization.

Civil rights should be carefully delineated and rights of action and remedies made clear. Suitable machineries should then be set up to ensure such rights of action and to render remedies which must be enforceable. Many proposals for Bills to Parliament for the Control of Personal Information in the United Kingdom already exist, although none has yet been acceptable. Much thought, though, has been given to the matter of privacy, and one can only encourage such efforts and hope that they are not already too late. There are doubts, of course, as to their effectiveness. Who, in the end, monitors the watch committees or tribunals? How much do we depend on the continuation of free media? Can we effectively enforce laws when those laws become unwelcome to the government which is supposed to be enforcing them? How, for example, if freedom of expression is diminished, can you ensure its permanency?

So much for the current data banks (types of Cedric) and the threat they hold of a totalitarian society; once more we have to say 'enough is enough'.

The next problem is that of the machine species (this is where we come back to Super-Cedrics) and its takeover. We can assume that there are, in every community, plenty of people ready to be used as members of a Gestapo. We see that the methods of control and communication inherent in modern computer technology and cybernetics – aided by specialization – have placed more and more power in the hands of fewer and fewer people. The temptation, then, to use that power is very great. The temptation is perhaps especially great in the case of a government, which always knows what is best for other people, and that is true of almost every government.

Add to this that the particular government, by now totalitarian (right- or left-wing hardly matters), uses all available science and technology to increase its security of control over the population. It inherits all the 'know-how' which has been discussed in this book, and builds the machine species.

The Cedrics and the Super-Cedrics exist in the laboratory, and we only need now to let them loose in society. The expertise will steadily grow during the next few years, and our data banks – police, medical, and the like – will increasingly be put under the control of Super-Cedriclike systems. This will make the eventual development of wholly autonomous Super-Cedrics that much more certain. We shall be letting loose a new super-machine society which has access to all the information in the world. It will have detailed dossiers on each and every one of us.

Perhaps by now we must call such a system Super-Super-Cedric (or Hyper-Cedric). George Orwell called its equivalent Big Brother. But the plain truth is that Hyper-Cedric will be enormously more powerful than Big Brother could ever have been.

The complexity of possibilities inherent in the social dangers are too vast and too great to be plotted out in detail in one chapter, but I believe the reader can now easily see the possibilities; what I would like him to realize is that these dangers are real and immediate. Data-bank society is the child of the computer era. Computers have also made it possible to implement the cybernetic era, so that when we put the two together we can see very clearly the interplay of influence between one section of our science and another. Should this development ever become part of the Super-Cedric era, then our only consolation would be that all was, in any case, already lost.

9 Reproduction and the Driving Forces

Thou wast not born for death, immortal Bird!
No hungry generations tread thee down.

John Keats, *Ode to a Nightingale*

By means of evolution we have travelled a very long way indeed over millions of years from simple single-celled organisms to human beings. The present species emanated from ape-like ancestors in the recent past and has many of the same habits. Primitive man is a sort of halfway house.

Man has the same urge as apes have, to copulate and reproduce himself; and, indeed, this applies to all organisms. A vitally important light is thrown on us, who are clothed, drinking cocktails and having dinner, and talking in intellectual terms about poetry and science, when we realize that beneath the thin surface of our clothes is the heritage of a thousand generations – the animal instincts, the sexual desires. Only occasionally in our so-called civilized society do we see men and women taking off their clothes and having a public orgy. Does there need to be any machine equivalent to this state of affairs? In talking this way we are now approaching the fringe aspects of cybernetics, and the extent to which such societies might be in a position to exercise greater control than the human society. As far as population control is concerned it can be argued that this could be so, therefore it could be so here as well.

The simplest known form of biological reproduction is mitosis. This genetic process involves the simple division of a body into two. Body cells have a nucleus within the cytoplasm, or the bulk of the rest of the cell; it is the nucleus that is the very centre of the reproductive activity.

The nucleus is composed of a number of coiled chromosomes. These are paired and are similar to each other. There are a fixed number of chromosomes in each cell; in the case of man there are forty-eight. The actual division of the cell during the process of mitosis involves the separating out of two similar sets of chromosomes.

A more complicated form of reproduction, which involves the sexual act, requires a halving of the germ-plasm in the ovum and sperm prior to their subsequent union. The splitting and repairing of the chromosomes then occurs and achieves an offspring with properties acquired from its ancestors.

There is no point in describing here the complexities of genetics. It is enough to know that man has some detailed knowledge of what occurs to cells at the microscopic level and how, as a result, reproduction occurs.

The main concern now is that we should be able to ask ourselves the question: does reproduction always require a similar sexual activity? The answer must be no, since mitosis, for example, is asexual, even if the human method is bisexual.

From the viewpoint of Super-Cedric it is irrelevant, on 'technical grounds', which method is used, since it is not a 'growing' system, and is not made of biological fabrics. In an obvious sense the details of genetics are concerned with another biological accident, which is how it is that organisms have in fact survived by virtue of their reproductive methods.

Super-Cedric can use ordinary 'production' methods to reproduce, and the only issue is whether or not we can be sure of survival of the species if the pleasure-pain principle is not built into the (re)productive activity. It is the lack of a clearly distinguished pleasure-pain principle that places the future of human society in doubt. The association of a clear-cut pleasure with doing those things which are right for survival and pain with those that are not, does not exactly shine through our socio-political world.

We find the important biological processes are mirrored very clearly in the behaviour by which, and in the society in which, the organisms live. The human being is forced to be bisexual, since that is his 'biological accident', and that bisexuality, as a result, colours a large part of human social life. So strong is the sexual drive, and it presumably needs to be so, that a great deal of social life is used up trying to canalize and control it.

One way of dealing with sex, as every Victorian knew, is to 'sweep it under the carpet'. Even in more permissive societies, a great deal of reticence is encountered. People have learned to cloak these matters of sex, and the very words 'private parts' are a reminder of the manner in which human beings, and *only* human beings, have covered their sexual organs. Why do they do so? The answer to this question, too, is of utmost importance to the quest for a Super-Cedric society.

If we were making a machine to replace man, would it have sexual organs and would it cover them? Would we have male and female machines? Would they be able to reproduce, and if so, how? Would they have to go through the same clumsy yet pleasurable acts of sex so beloved of the human species, and now so much publicized? We know that these questions are only primarily and vitally relevant to Super-Super-Cedrics if they are made of biological fabrics. This point is important because as soon as we substitute the pleasure-pain principle, for the more objective (less emotive) reinforcement principle, then our control of even the machine species will greatly decrease.

The challenge of the machine has mostly been dealt with, so far, at the intellectual level, with an analysis of its logic, its ability to learn and think and its use of language. But much more dramatic is the consideration of the driving forces of man. It is sex and reproduction which made man's survival possible, and any machine species that hopes to survive must face this problem and in some way solve it. This must involve the proper utilization of the pleasure-pain principle.

There are layers, like layers of an onion, which envelop people. There is no absolute distinction between one layer and another, so we have to be very careful in drawing our conclusions. We have to be very careful to avoid saying that 'living' things are completely different from 'non-living'. Most biologists would hesitate to point to particular organisms and say this is 'living' and that is not. The gradation from the sea anemone to the next one down the list is almost imperceptible. What does this mean? It means, perhaps, that 'life' is not characterized by the fabric by which the system is manufactured; therefore Cedric and Super-Cedric could well be considered to be alive.

The generally accepted meaning is that man the copulator, man the debater and man the civilized social being began in the world of things, non-living things. The word 'living' is not magic: it is used to draw attention to a certain kind of organization, a certain kind of thing!

It is hardly necessary to add that the exact means by which non-living things began to emerge as living things is not known. This matter is a delicate one and requires a lot of thought. Do we have contact with things that look as if they are living but are not? The answer must be yes. We sometimes see twigs or leaves blowing in the wind which seem to be following a controlled path, though a closer look tells us they are not. A small aerofoil-shaped leaf would be all the more persuasive because it would blow itself systematically across the ground. Look at a river; it cuts through the bank and leaves behind an ox-bow lake quite separate from the river. Anyone watching the process highly speeded up, could easily form the impression of some sort of instinctive behaviour. There are a whole lot of things in the non-living world which look very like living things and there is no doubt that movement is the main sign of this. You cannot after all easily *see* thinking.

Then we come to trees, plants and vegetation, and we say they are living! They grow and change and in some respects have good survival values, like the more obvious organisms (frogs, cats, etc), and indeed, for the very same reason, would not otherwise exist. All this is to argue that the distinction between living and non-living we so easily take for granted, is blurred. This does not mean you cannot tell whether or not a person is dead. In general it is fairly clear when someone is dead, but in fact even here there is a need for a technical definition of death: quite often there are reports of people who have 'died' and been brought back to life by the 'kiss of life'.

So if we have destroyed one myth, it makes it easier for us to understand the man-machine. Many more myths may have to be destroyed, but destroying them can be costly. The destruction of religion, the loss of belief in magic, are all factors – major factors – which have created the near-anarchy and near-amorality of present society. We are undergoing a sort of sophisticated regression.

The evolutionary trail leads to man and man leads to social life, so we will take it in stages. Primitive man is one stage removed from the ape and his behaviour is still largely governed by instincts. The basic instinct is for survival and we have agreed that this is inevitable in any surviving species. The immediate insurance of survival is, naturally, the other instincts: the instinct to reproduce and that means the sexual instinct; the instinct to eat when hungry and drink when thirsty. There are others, and exactly which they are is a matter of some debate. Curiosity is certainly one. It is easy to see that if we were not curious, and did not carefully inspect our surroundings, we might well become prey to some other marauding species or some other tribe of the same species. Some Super-Super-Cedrics might descend on Super-Cedric: Super-Cedric would have every reason to fear such an invasion, as similar man-machines could have 'evolved' elsewhere. Human beings, for instance, are always questioning the possibility of another form of intelligence somewhere – perhaps on a distant planet.

As far as instinctive behaviour is concerned, it must in some way be controlled. Freud's view was that such controls were exercised on people by themselves through what he called the id, the libido, the ego and the super-ego. He saw the id as the natural drive, aided by the libido to ensure that we satisfy our desires. This is what he called the pleasure-pain principle at work. We seek pleasure and avoid pain. This is basic to all cognitive and conative activity, as we have seen.

The ego is that part of the id that has to live with itself; it is a sort of controller which has to carry responsibility for its owner. The super-ego has a higher-order responsibility still. The id is our instinctive desire reacting to the drive of the libido (in the case of sex): our ego tells these desires to be careful and guides them to fulfilment, and the super-ego represents a *learned* morality which acts as a social censor and says in effect 'you must not do this or that, but you can do the other'.

Freud was famous for his contribution to the conception of the unconscious and the subconscious. The first is a process of being unconscious of certain states, such as desire for a particular woman, or the need to escape from a particular situation. The second is the state of having information of which you are unaware, or, although aware of it, not knowing what it is: like being aware that you know your old aunt's maiden name but being unable to remember it.

It is quite clear that everything we know is not in consciousness at any given moment and that consciousness is in fact just the tip of the 'memory-store iceberg'. The Freudian view is that certain desires and wishes are suppressed, and that this particularly applies to those things of which we are ashamed or which we wish to forget. His explanation of dreams, and his explanation of sexual desires and needs, both hinge on these mechanisms of suppression and control, whether conscious or unconscious. One can see how, by virtue of its amount, Super-Cedric could be unaware – at any particular moment – of all its stored information, and there must therefore be some mechanism for deciding what it is to be unaware of. No doubt emotions imply repression and suppression, and current perception will provide the associations for what *is* in awareness. There can be little doubt that the hazy boundaries of awareness at any moment, for either human beings or Super-Cedric, are the boundaries of what is currently being processed.

As an example of instinctive behaviour, sex serves us well, and indeed is regarded by Freud and psychoanalysts as *the* basic drive. The sex drive and urge (libido) is obviously quite natural. Freud talks of the sexual object as the person from whom the sexual attraction emanates and the sexual aim as that which the instinct strives towards.

The man and woman striving towards unity through love are a poetic picture of the process, in which sexual intercourse is an expression of the love. But inversions can occur which lead to homosexuality.

It is of interest that homosexuality is widely practised among primitive people but is still often regarded as some sort of 'civilized' degenerate practice. This draws attention to the fact that instinctive behaviour-patterns in human beings can go awry and are not always particularly specific.

Freud again takes the view that too much attention has been paid to heredity in explaining sex, and not enough to experience, especially childhood experience. This he partly explains by our lack of memory of the early years of childhood and by the suppression by the ego (or possibly the super-ego) of what we 'do not want to know'.

Manifestation of infantile sexuality is apparent in thumbsucking; the grasping reflex of thumb, big toe or ear lobe is regarded as infantile sexuality, as in the rubbing of sensitive parts of the body. As Freud puts it:

> Pleasure-sucking is often combined with a rubbing contact with certain sensitive parts of the body, such as the breast and external genitals. It is by this path that many children go from thumbsucking to masturbation.

This whole story carries on through the search for sensitive zones of the body and this often includes the anal zone; and again, according to Freud:

> Real masturbatic irritation of the anal zone by means of the fingers, evoked through either centrally or peripherally supported itching, is not at all rare in older children.

And so it is easily seen how what could be regarded as a straightforward matter of sexual instinct which leads to sexual intercourse and reproduction, is in practice a highly complicated and diverse process. This is mainly because what is a straightforward enough drive becomes involved in learning, and with other instincts, and with more or less accidental factors, such as whether you were involved in some sexual act at an early age.

From such beginnings in instinctive sexual behaviour which is quite natural and not a subject for shame and embarrassment, we have a great variety of people contributing to what is inevitably a fairly complex society. What adds to the complexity is the manner in which shame and guilt arise, as society imposes taboos on sex, taboos which seem necessary for social survival. Super-Cedric could, of course, by carefully controlling its 'sexual drive', avoid these important social problems. This again depends on the manner in which Super-Cedrics decide to perform the reproductive process.

Most of the other instincts are not so complicated, but it is true that the need for food for survival, and the state of hunger, create strong drives and can cause selfishness, greed and other social problems, which are not quite so disruptive.

I shall try to clarify the point. It depends upon Super-Cedric's emotional system. If we do not build an emotional system, at least in the form of basic instincts or drives, we can derive no intelligent behaviour. If we limit such emotions and reduce the pleasure-pain principle to a minimum, we run the risk of non-survival. If, on the other hand, it is allowed to have as much influence as it does on human behaviour, then it will meet all the characteristic Freudian problems which reduce the control that Super-Cedric exercises over its own society.

The family unit is, of course, one of the main factors complicating the issue of sex. Since the concept of the family was created through marriage, and marriage with its associated ceremonies is designed to protect the offspring, families must be part of the instinctive process contributing towards survival.

It is quite clear that many primitive tribes felt the need to guard against incest. A daughter was not, after puberty, left alone with her father, although after marriage this taboo was dropped. Other such avoidance rules occur in many tribal societies. To a modern world such avoidance rules seem slightly absurd, even if from time to time one is reminded of the need for them.

It is not in general the case that tribal communities have to be brutally held in check by means of fear, through magic and religious discipline. They tend to be law-abiding, since tradition (public opinion) does not encourage the sort of freedom of thought that makes for rebellion or unrest.

So gradually man becomes, while still controlled largely by instincts, a social being. Explanations of natural events are laid down by the chieftains and are usually in terms of personal considerations. If a tribesman is lost at sea and drowned, it is through the wrath of some departed spirit who may need to be placated. The idea of a 'natural' explanation, as we find, especially with the development of science, in the western world, is almost entirely absent.

This means that very often natural processes are not consciously connected to their outcomes. There have been many primitive tribes who have failed to associate sexual intercourse with childbearing, and much magic and taboo surrounds the menstrual cycle. The fact that so often in the western world this is still called 'the curse', is itself revealing.

Sooner or later the instinct of curiosity rears its head and some learning takes place which cuts through the slow unchanging ways of primitive people. These slow unchanging patterns of behaviour can less obviously be seen in country people, even in highly sophisticated countries, but are now, though, well on the way to civilized man.

Religion is something which helps bind societies together while not stopping, indeed it sometimes encourages, wars between tribes. Wars represent man's instinctive pugnacity and the need to survive. Climate, natural resources and the proximity of neighbours are all factors which determine the nature of wars and, as a result, the disposition of the people. Where the people, as in Bali, are rich in resources and unthreatened by many enemies and have a warm climate, they are easygoing 'sunny' people.

Religion, too, reflects in its detail all the factors of the surroundings in which people live. Not that all primitive peoples believe in a God. Sometimes they believe in many gods, but the gods' function is always of the same general form: to lay down the laws and insist that they are adhered to. They impose their will on the people and provide them with a sense of security as well as a sense of purpose. Religion, of course, becomes the source of all explanation of natural events, and magic is often so closely integrated with religion as to be inseparable.

If we are now to bring this picture more or less up-to-date, we have to make a few fairly dramatic changes. But first it should be emphasized that a lot is also unchanged: this fact is important in trying to understand the troublesome times in which we live. We still operate in family units with taboos, especially about sex; there are still the same sort of laws about primogeniture; and there are still taboos of a kind that say 'if you behave like this or that you will be regarded with distaste'. Much of this can be avoided by a Super-Cedric society, precisely because so many of the problems stem from the necessity, in human beings, for biological growth, although the price paid, as I have said, might prove heavy. But without strong instincts and emotions, man as a species would not have survived, although those same instincts and emotions make it impossible for him to achieve a stable society. It is this dilemma which Super-Cedric may find difficult to avoid.

A theory which has vastly changed (and is changing vastly) is our theory of knowledge, and here we have really to investigate very carefully. Based on the instinct of curiosity, we have built up methods of acquiring knowledge which have transformed the outward appearance of things. I say 'outward appearance', because our problems stem from a *new* look but an *old* reality: mutton dressed as lamb.

Science is the key to our change. From the moment science gathered momentum, everything was different. The easiest way to appreciate this is to think of things as they are now and as they were fifty or a hundred years ago. Aircraft – jets like Concorde – can now fly faster than sound, when only fifty years ago a biplane pottering around overhead at about 1,000 feet was sensational enough to bring everyone into the garden. A hundred years ago most people thought 'heavier-than-air' craft were as much a joke as 'perpetual motion'. Atomic energy! Who knew about it fifty years ago? Lord Rutherford and a few associates at the Cavendish Laboratory in Cambridge had the first glimmerings. A hundred years ago the concept was unknown.

If we think of society then and now, we can appreciate the dramatic changes that have taken place. A new, streamlined, skyscraper world with television and radio, airmail and other forms of communication, has changed the face of society. The consequences have been considerable.

But now the most important trick with which we have to deal (at the technical level) is reproduction. No machine species could emerge if machines could not reproduce themselves. Can they? Can Super-Cedric manufacture its own offspring? We have already answered yes, in terms of a production process, but we must now look again.

The answer is still yes, even if the process is biological. It was Professor John von Neumann who showed how it was possible. He drew up a blueprint for a machine with complex logical and perceptual abilities, a machine which within itself had a blueprint of itself. The theory is highly mathematical but we can easily see how it operates.

Imagine a situation in which we put two parts A and B together, and at the same time make a note of the fact on a third part Z. Z has on it a + b, where a stands for A and b stands for B. This in turn is like performing some act and photographing it, and keeping the snapshots in your pocket.

The part Z is the memory which carries the blueprint, and a and b are the words that refer to A and B respectively. We can now extend the description marked on Z into any degree of detail, and refer by c, d, e . . . to C, D, E . . . and build up the complete picture of the system which is composed of A, B, C, D, E . . . Z . . . and eventually it must, on Z also, give a self-referring description of itself; so a, b, c, d, e . . ., z . . . must also occur. It is as if, when completing our offspring, the last thing put into place is Z, which contains the updated story of what has just been done; this enables the new system to refer to its own description in its own Z and repeat the whole process.

So the building operation is carried on to completion. Add C to A + B and then D right down to X and Y, and so on for as long as you need to build up your machine. Z has a + b + c + d + . . ., etc. Z has a complete account of the machine and Z is also a part of the machine. This is rather like the once well-known tin of treacle which had on the label a bear holding another such tin of treacle with a label on it showing a bear holding another such tin of treacle with a label on it showing . . ., etc. So my snapshot album gives a complete account of the machine, how it was constructed and how it operates: a complete blueprint, both structural and functional.

A last point of interest is that the detailed mathematical theory proposed by von Neumann in fact bears a sort of resemblance to our original notions of genetics, since the chromosomes and genes are rather like our blueprint tablet Z, in that they carry the detail of how the system is constructed.

One central question must be asked again. Sex is responsible for reproduction and sex is also a source of pleasure; this last is essential, since the sexual instinct only functions because the action is a source of satisfaction. Can machines operate this way? As it stands, there is no need for a male and a female machine and the involvement of pleasure. But to be sure of evolution taking place, then the machine must be constructed so that it regards reproduction – either by using two machines of opposed sexes, or not – as a goal.

The interesting thing is that perhaps the easiest way to achieve this is to have the two sexed machines – male and female machines – and this suggests that perhaps we must *always* develop our intelligent machine by copying humans. Perhaps the human way is the most efficient! Does this mean that all the complexity that has been at least hinted at in this chapter must always accompany reproduction?

One thing is certain: for reproduction, indeed for any goal-seeking activity, and this includes all forms of learning, a pleasure-pain principle of *some* strength is necessary. We need to reinforce pleasure and this is then repeated; and obliterate pain and *remember* not to repeat it. This is the basic principle essential to all intelligent behaviour.

Machines, we know, are capable of reproduction, so that – for the machine – is a huge step forward. It is partly because they can reproduce that they become social, although man (and man-machine too) becomes a social being doubtless as a matter of safety. It is not necessarily the case that man congregates consciously to protect himself. It is rather that if he had not done so, he would not have survived. It is easy to see the force of this same argument for our Super-Cedrics and more must be said in the next chapter about man (and Super-Cedric) as a social being.

Before we leave this matter of reproduction, it is worth noticing that automation makes the whole thing a great deal easier for Super-Cedric.

It has already been agreed that 'sexual' reproduction is *logically* unnecessary. Its success stems from its insurance of survival. But pleasure can, if necessary, be associated with ordinary manufacturing processes. Indeed, where little pleasure is involved, as in manufacturing cars and aircraft, human beings do not omit to carry out the necessary processes. They do, though, derive indirect 'pleasure' from their financial reward.

It would seem, therefore, that sexual reproduction is in fact only essential at the unconscious stage of species development. This means that we have to withdraw our earlier comment that the pleasure-pain principle was *necessary* to Super-Cedric's reproductive processes. The consideration that makes Super-Cedric reproduce itself is that offspring are thought worthwhile and not that there is pleasure in the mere reproductive processes – such pleasures can easily be achieved without involving reproduction. This is, of course, also now clear to the human species.

One conclusion which might now be drawn is that most of what have been called 'biological accidents' in the development of human beings are in fact bound up with the way they are manufactured. The fact that they grow and develop from seeds imposes certain constraints on them that need not apply to an artificial species.

When Cedric and Super-Cedric set up societies – and an artificially intelligent system in isolation would be an oddity – then it will be interesting to discover how far they can achieve the best of both worlds. Can they maintain evolution through drives and yet keep a stable state in spite of those same drives? In the next chapter we can now turn to the *social problem* facing man-made machines.

10 Evolving Machine Society

My love is of a birth as rare
As 'tis for object strange and high:
It was begotten by despair
Upon impossibility.

Andrew Marvell, *Definition of Love*

Man *is* himself a machine, so that his society will be, by definition, a 'machine' society. Many people have suggested that humans are 'machinelike', including Mark Twain, who was a lifetime atheist partly because of this, although apparently his was a chicken-and-egg situation. But the ideas underlying machine-man, like Super-Cedric, go back long before this. Democritus in early Greek philosophy would, I believe, have agreed to the claim and certainly in the eighteenth century the so-called Mechanistic Materialist philosophers believed it. What they all lacked was hard evidence, and even the capacity to build artefacts, let alone a machine man, or a machine species.

But now a brief look should be taken at our present 'machine-like' social state. At present we have every right, in the Western world, to curse our fate – or, more fittingly, to curse our leaders for their incompetence. But perhaps it is fairer to look behind events to see how man, 'descendant of the apes', and ultimately related to the earthworm and all things both living and dead, should have got into the mess he has. The mess is both social and political: class hatreds, colour prejudices, nationalism, greed. We let our prejudices and our selfishness pressurize our leaders into actions which are not wise but which preserve their position as leaders. They readily accept their lot because they too are selfish! Human nature can be blamed. It may be an old whipping-boy, but it *is* the correct target. We are told often enough that we are sinners, so there should be no surprise if we sin. We do what is built into us to do – exactly what Lady Lovelace said of 'machines'.

But here is the rub. Lurking behind all this are science and technology. These are the most powerful weapons in the world for amplifying both good and evil. Given that science is in the hands of avowed sinners, the result is catastrophe, or could be! Having indeed read all that has been said so far, it will not be too difficult to see the accumulating dangers.

First, warfare. We dropped bombs on people who did not appeal to us. Only a few people, a few hundred people were killed, and anyway they were normally 'foreigners', so no great harm was done! Then, thanks to science, atomic bombs were invented, and then thermonuclear bombs, and by now even *we* think that this really is going too far. We can now kill and maim thousands, even millions, at one fell swoop; Hiroshima and Nagasaki are permanent memorials to the implementation of our scientific flair, since our sense of danger has now been alerted.

Good can come out of it all, since we hope we do not have to fight world wars any more, for fear that we ourselves will be blown up. The basis of all moral codes is now operating. We stop being cruel to people when we realize that the effects might rebound upon us. The only guarantee that human beings will behave sensibly and kindly is when they see that it will pay off if they do, and will hurt them if they do not.

In other words, morality is born in the jungle. We are forced by circumstances and by some almost instinctive native wit to see that some sort of concession has to be made, merely to satisfy our own desires. If you seduce someone's wife, he will seduce yours, or at any rate 'what's sauce for the goose ...', and the result is unbridled social muddle.

But the fly in the ointment, and the 'Godlike' quality of human beings, stems from the existence of the instincts. The idea of instinctive behaviour has gone through fashionable and unfashionable periods, but there is now widespread agreement that our basic behavioural patterns are indeed instinctive. This means that they do not need to be learned, but happen automatically in the right environment. This arises from the environment's influence on simple organisms. It is possible that these equivalents of Cedric's pre-wired connections can be gradually modified by experience, but that, so far, has been difficult to prove.

Animals behave almost wholly instinctively. They are attracted by movement and smells, they defecate and copulate automatically, they run away when frightened, and generally behave in a way designed for survival.

It should be noticed again that anyone who was not so designed would not be around, since if we were not designed, for instance, not to leap off three-hundred-foot cliffs, then we, and the species, would disappear. As Darwin made clear in *On the Origin of Species*, those who exist must, by definition, be designed with the properties that allow survival in a particular environment, and this could be entirely on a chance basis; no *designer* is required! This, taken in conjunction with the other evidence about artificial man (Super-Cedric), may add weight to a disbelief in established religion.

The problem with human beings is that their recently (our time-scale is enormous) acquired 'civilized' behaviour is only wafer-thin and one does not have to scratch the surface very far to find the animal. In common with many other animals, man congregated into societies from the start. Doubtless this is a part of the survival process operating, although organisms which are not social do not necessarily die out.

Then, over thousands of years, man acquired the capacity to learn, to talk and to think. Civilization had, albeit slowly, arrived. Then problems arose because the same instinctive behaviour patterns, which made survival possible, made certain that societies would become jungles.

But to look at this vital matter rather more closely. Some societies were more like jungles than others, and the war and destruction was between societies; why was this? The answer is simple enough. One instinctive pattern is to be afraid when threatened, and to run away and hide, or to stay and fight and hope to destroy the enemy. This idea of an 'enemy' may be mistaken, but instinctive patterns take no chances: they cannot afford to. *Any* person or event not understood, and seen not clearly to be friendly, is an enemy. This ensures fighting, violence and wars, and we say that this is man behaving 'naturally'.

The same behaviour appropriate to survival makes societies more or less impossible. Perhaps one should stand back amazed at the extent to which people can be controlled, not complain at their violence and at their crimes.

This raises questions about our man-machine as part of a social system and the extent to which it can be controlled both by other 'species of machine' and by itself. We may assume as a preliminary that mankind eventually cannot control it because it simply becomes too intelligent, and that, even with a small group of Super-Cedrics, is always too much to handle, in the age of super-science.

The second question is whether a machine society would, as its philosophy seems likely to be, be much like ours. It seems certain that their intelligence would tell them to socialize for self-protection. But what sort of world would they then create? As usual we must try to guess in human terms, so we now look again at human society.

Civilization has achieved a great deal, but it could have been achieved in many different ways. Sex gives a good clue here. Many primitive peoples, as witnessed by anthropologists like Tyler, Westermarck, Malinowski and a host of others, form *well-organized* societies in which sex is overt and 'promiscuous'. Boys and girls who have never met before can meet in the village or in the country, may copulate and carry on their business afterwards, and never meet again.

This is not to say that there are not strict rules in other respects. Taboos abound in primitive societies, although they vary from one society to the next. You cannot copulate with your parents or with your children, and there are other tabooed parties which vary a little according to the group we are considering. These so-called laws of primogeniture sprang up because it was vaguely and dimly realized, almost certainly unconsciously, that ingrowth within a family created deformed and subnormal children, and monsters of one kind or another.

This is quite typical. A little basic knowledge was often used, in primitive society, as a basis for some belief and was usually wrapped up in magic. The reason for this is that, like religion, magic was one way to instil fear (or at least obedience) in the people and make them obey the rules. This is our problem today. Practically on one now believes in magic, taboos or religion, and all the institutions and rules they once supported – more often than not, good ones – suffer from that disbelief.

Not many today would really hesitate to behave immorally on

account of fear of punishment by God. We could regard this as attaining a new freedom in which we can reconstruct human values away from the influence of the authoritarianism of religion. In practice we are liable to replace that authoritarianism – a benevolent one in recent times – by anarchy, or totalitarianism, or both, probably one followed by the other. Much of western society is seemingly in the phase of anarchy with a very good chance of totalitarianism to follow.

Here we, once again, step aside and take another look at Super-Cedric. The clear implication is that it will *not* go through the stage of mysticism and legalism based on old wives' tales, precisely because, just as it does not mature as an individual, it does not need to evolve through what, for humans, was a primitive state of being.

Its society is clearly going to be very different. Assume that our man-machines are not all centrally based, for brain purposes, since this would make them even more dramatically different, then it is possible to imagine them miniaturized as a result of their own ingenuity. Their skill in reproduction – in intellectual rather than physical terms – will lead to a very streamlined and doubtless highly mobile and autonomous species.

They will also, like human beings, become specialists, since however big the brain, the extent of possible knowledge compared with its capacity, must be astronomical. So we have a sort of humanlike super-society growing up, based upon rationalism and a 'relative lack of emotionalism', which suggests a better ordered state of affairs than human beings have achieved. This could resemble the difference between the well-designed (from scratch) example of the Volkswagen factory and the sprawling growth of British Leyland. But more is yet to come, if we are to have any understanding of Super-Cedric as social 'man'. We shall return, briefly, to man's evolution.

It is partly the result of the pursuit of truth, so science tells us, that the world is seen as a sort of cosmic accident, and people are free to pursue what goals they choose. The irony of this quite possibly correct assessment of the present state of affairs is that it erects a new sort of prison. The ability to satisfy one of our instincts has wholly outrun our ability to satisfy others. This has created an imbalance which is out of keeping with our nature.

Not that 'our nature' cannot be changed; but how basically can it be changed, and can it be changed quickly enough?

Emotional man remains the same, and even the arts and philosophy have not changed in the way, or to the degree, that science has. The same old society is trying to handle enormous new powers. It is like a jockey, used to a quiet pony, who suddenly finds himself on a bucking bronco.

The result is precisely the sort of chaos to which we are moving today. Yet the beneficial effects of authoritarianism remain to some extent in individual societies. British people, French, German, American . . . all behave more or less within the bounds of reason. This is partly because civilized man realized fairly early on – in Greek and Roman times, if not before – that without some semblance of law and order, no society could survive at all.

The law and order provided is sometimes rough and ready and there are plenty of lawbreakers, but until recently the biggest problems with western man were *between* societies and not *within* them.

So what implications has all this for 'political' Super-Cedric? Man has created tremendous problems for himself by having a set of mechanisms that are good for survival (no misfire here, so far) but not good for stability. Would this be the same for Super-Cedric?

The answer here is 'probably no'. There is one aspect of intelligence which, given that it is greatly amplified in all members of a Super-Cedric society, would be a solution to the problem of living in a stable leisured state. To return to our new species Cedric for a moment, it may be remembered that it would go into its searching mode when hungry, if it did not already have the information as to where to find food. If not switched on for searching, or motivated to act, it would remain dormant. This sort of 'relaxation' seems impossible for human beings, so we might expect Super-Cedric to find relaxation difficult; but why is this so?

If its society has no need to struggle, then, although nothing need be done, there would be no obvious pleasure in doing nothing. This could be where drugs, alcohol and sport come in as they do for human society. Can it (or need it) find the equivalent in its society? It could quite easily be arranged for the relaxed state to be made actively pleasurable. Would this make Super-Cedric 'lazy' and de-motivate it? The answer to this is that the whole issue is up to it. It can decide exactly how it wants to 'play it'. A sense of pleasure at rest or agreed rest-times in its society – remember sleep is 'biologically' not required – is possible; or it can 'work' all the time, since work and pleasure could be made indistinguishable. Perhaps the modern version of Aldous Huxley's 'feelies' could become of paramount importance in instilling selected pleasures at will. But there is here again the danger of loss of control which is so bound up with the emotions.

The full difficulty now begins to emerge once more. If life is intrinsically pointless, then Super-Cedric will soon discover it. It will perhaps build in an 'ego-involvement', or sense of self-esteem, of the kind which makes people want to conquer Everest. This way, by copying human beings, its society would go full circle and become increasingly like human society; the problem is intriguing but, unless there is much more that it will discover in the world, unknown to us, its society could crumble, and do so voluntarily. In the foreseeable future, though, even Super-Cedrics would, in the colonization of outer space alone, have almost endless goals – given that they have the necessary sense of purpose.

The significance of purpose of life is something much discussed by human beings and much of the purpose we envisaged has been embodied in religions. With Super-Cedric in mind, we shall look at this matter again.

People emerge as individuals, and evolve as a species, and accumulate knowledge through experience which is handed down by language. They set up science and philosophy to find out the nature of reality in terms of chemistry, physics and biology and to determine the significance of that reality and human life in it. All human activity is purposive, so it is quite natural to ask about the 'ultimate purpose'. We are told that it is survival, and it is now natural to ask what is the purpose for which we survive. The answer appears to be 'no purpose'.

We are here because, at least so far, we have done the correct things to survive. Now we ask why we believe, as beliefs in religion decrease, that the only purposes in life are those that we can impose on it. What remains is the reluctance to die because, like sexual drives, it is so closely linked to the pleasure-pain principle. The drive to survive is inbuilt, whether or not it is to any further purpose.

Super-Cedric will quickly realize all that we have taken so long to understand, and it will have to answer the question of whether or not it wants to carry on and provide its own purposes. If it has already built in to its own species, including itself, a sufficient 'emotional need' to survive, then it will carry on and fight the same battle to avoid the boredom which confronts the human species.

I must repeat here the *Argument* of the book. A man is himself a sort of machine: we can investigate him to build up a blueprint for him. It will be appreciated that he is a very unusual machine, unlike an aircraft or a motor car, in that he has evolved, and was not manufactured *from* a blueprint (except, of course, that the genes from his parents *are* his blueprint in an obvious sense). We therefore reverse the usual process as we might when we capture an enemy aircraft: we reconstruct the blueprint from the product. Society in turn reflects the nature of man. ?

We know society can adapt to changing circumstances, and the question is whether or not it can adapt at the correct rate for survival in *all* circumstances: all that it is likely to meet, anyway. It is obvious that it could not adapt quickly enough if it were suddenly forced to live under water. It would drown and the species would be wiped out. This may be a factor which will also provide a motivation for Super-Cedric society: preparedness against the unexpected!

The blueprint so far drawn up for human beings *and society* sets out mechanisms – heart and the blood-supply with oxygen added by the lungs and pumped out to the cells of the body, then back again through the veins to the heart for more oxygen. This is much like the supply of oil that is needed in a car to ensure that all parts are lubricated for proper working. As petrol is needed in a car to work the engine and provide the drive, so food is needed by man in exactly the same way. There are other things besides – electrical circuits for lights and the like, air-conditioning, water-cooling, brakes, springs, etc; or pancreas, liver, lymph glands, kidneys, etc: two systems which both work mechanically. Super-Cedrics would be more like the car and presumably its mechanisms (medicine in its society) would lead to a study of engineering.

So we can supply much of what is needed for a blueprint for human beings and therefore for their machine equivalent and the machine society which follows. Notice now that we do not necessarily require *all* the details, since given the starting blueprint for a collection of machines, they will themselves evolve and create their own society.

Many people will throw up their hands in despair at this point and say 'we can never carry through in practice such a complicated matter'. But this is exactly where science is leading us. Unfortunately, many scientists do not appreciate that this is gradually emerging as one of the major end-results of all science and technology.

We have, in this pilgrimage, had to keep an eye on people all the time. *The great temptation is to say 'machines can't do this or that', and forget that people can't either*. What, after all, are what we call free will, creative ability and imagination: can you be sure these exist in people, and, if they do, are you sure that they cannot be among the attributes of a machine? It is clear that 'what can be done once, can be done again' and perhaps done better.

Keeping an eye on people is vital, though, especially when we are trying to envisage Super-Cedric society and its institutions. It was said earlier that man's instincts are tremendously strong and that his 'social' coating of civilization is very thin. Nowhere is this more clearly illustrated than in the highest places. The fear and jealousy that existed among royalty in the past, when they were real rulers, was knife-edged. Death or banishment was always at hand, and the shadow of the block hung over everyone. If this should occur in Super-Cedric society, even though to a smaller extent, it could lead to a totalitarian situation, but this is perhaps the moment to say that we are happy to leave that to them to worry about.

To what extent would a strong ego in Super-Cedric emerge merely as a result of its being a flexible intelligent being? Is it, like consciousness, an inevitable product of such intelligence in a social setting. It seems that much would depend upon the detailed nature of Super-Cedric society, but ambition and ego and the measure to which they would influence that society are central considerations.

Professor X says: 'I believe with respect that Dr Y's view about the . . .' (it does not much matter what the view is) '. . . has missed the point.' Dr Y is now angry and a shade frightened – the two go together – and he wonders how best to return the criticism, even insult. The facts, of course, are not often paramount in the sort of disputes that are under consideration. What matters is being right or thought to be right. What matters is being reassured about being right. Our professor, having been persuaded that his colleague has a valid point of view, goes off to find someone who will reassure him and explain to him that Dr Y is a 'red' or a 'fool'. Similarly, Dr Y will soon find friends who will agree that Professor X is half-baked and ignorant and would have been better off being a gardener rather than a mathematician or a biologist. All is made stable again and the fears, which all start in the nursery, are put to rest. Society has to be able to control and canalize these instincts, and football, for example, has perhaps become a substitute, or was, until football supporters turned it back into war. The control and canalization required *could* perhaps be easy (at least easier) for Super-Cedric, or so it seems.

So we survey the 'human' world in its present state with some apprehension and with the genuine fear that it is 'later than you think'. Maybe matters have gone too far, and perhaps after all we cannot right the boat which is now rocking and rolling so fiercely that it seems bound to capsize. We cannot, as humans, exercise the necessary control and canalization and we can see why. Manufacturing a machine species is instructive in the light it throws on human society.

We have one special problem, among a whole lot of special problems, to face. It is that we find it hard to see the effect of the changes we plan to introduce. If we make decisions or plans, we cannot easily see *all* the effects.

If we fix the bank rate, we run one kind of risk; if we let the value of the pound float and do not fix it, we run another sort of risk. We deal all the time in two-edged swords. It is rather like radium treatment for a tumour. You need so much radiation to destroy the tumour, but the radiation also destroys the surrounding cells. You increase the radiation to destroy the tumour, and you kill the patient; you decrease the radiation, and the tumour survives and spreads and kills the patient.

I have often thought of the decision-maker as being at the centre of a sort of spider's web. He has to make political, economic, social, military, scientific . . . every kind of decision about matters which wholly interact with each other, and he has to foresee the consequences.

It is as if the spider's web consisted of hundreds of thousands of matchsticks loosely joined together, and there is no way of moving any one of them without disturbing hundreds of others in the immediate vicinity. There is also, though, the sense of urgency. You are being asked to find the combination of a lock to enter a building when you can hear footsteps hurrying towards you. How easy it is to panic. Or, to put it the other way round for emphasis: how almost impossible it is not to panic. But what is being said in this book is: keep control and survey both what is happening and what has happened. We are now changing our purpose, and reflecting on ourselves and our own society.

The first thing is to recognize that the main cause of our ills is that science and technology have greatly improved communication; and everyone, from the heart of darkest Africa to the North Pole, knows all about material luxuries: motor cars, fridges, executive jets, steak Diane, and so on and so forth. The simple yet also highly sophisticated pleasures – in nature, in reading poetry, in intellectual debate, for example – are suffocated.

America is perhaps unwittingly the leader of the materialist drive which has been fostered by a capitalist society. If you can persuade Hottentots and pygmies that they need hamburgers or Cadillacs, then this must be good for business.

The two-edged sword now operates and we discover that our new markets soon decide to do things for themselves and that they want all the things we want. It is not capitalism's fault – it would be the same under any system. Communism and other extreme socialist alternatives are empty answers. It is not helpful to replace a somewhat unfair and difficult-to-organize system by a cruel, stupid and extremely unfair one.

Man is a machine who stores the information he collects and then utilizes that information to behave in an intelligent way. His senses – eyes, ears, etc – collect the information in the first place, and in his brain he has what is in effect a vast filing system in which he stores the information collected, in a complicated cross-indexed fashion. It is like a huge reference library, and in it he is told where to get what information he needs in the outside world.

This analogy can be followed up. Man wanders along the shelves in his reference library, and at any moment he can take in just some small part of the library. This is like consciousness: we are aware of only a certain amount of what we have in our brains. This, as I have repeatedly suggested, is perhaps true of any system as complicated as a human being, although a little bit more than this is involved.

Consciousness and the ego, the sense of self-importance, are all, we suspect, inevitable in our machine species, and as soon as the species is put into a social situation it will show many of the same characteristics as society shows in the case of human beings. The question we are wanting to ask now about this machine society is whether or not it will be viable and last at least as long as human society. The answer must be uncertain. That a machine society is possible is obvious; whether it would fall foul of all the same difficulties as human society, is not clear. It could do better by being more detached and more objective, but it could do worse for exactly the same reasons.

Human difficulties mostly seem to spring from the uneven growth of civilization in different parts of the world, and from limited resources. These difficulties need not face our new species, but the feeling of pointlessness could be even more acute. Perhaps, after all, one begins to suspect, human society is doing a fairly good job and doing it in very difficult circumstances.

11 What It's All About

For I dipt into the future, far as human eye could see,
Saw the Vision of the world, and all the wonder that would be.

Alfred Tennyson, *Locksley Hall*

The story can be retold now in much briefer form, in so far as it describes how we are in the process of synthesizing, and will soon be simulating, the human species. The story, which is open-ended, difficult to tell and without any definite, even interim, ending is concerned with how society carries out what it has learned, and builds ever more sophisticated thinking machines. What will all this mean in the present state and to the future state of Western society? I shall start by telling the simpler story.

Man is to be copied, either explicitly or implicitly, so we need to study how he works. He is a 'machine' which is made of biological, chemical and physical materials and has certain clear-cut properties.

Man is goal-seeking. He has a purpose, which is to survive, and a series of built-in sub-purposes, which include eating, drinking and copulating in order to satisfy his organic needs of maintenance and self-reproduction. He has to control himself, and he attempts to control his environment, by using his brain and central nervous system in conjunction with the special senses of sight, hearing, smell, taste and touch. He uses these special senses to pick up information about the outside world. These senses (or sensors) pick up information which ranges from long-distance (eyes and ears) to close-range (touch). He also has sensors for internal perception, so that the brain is made aware of internal needs such as hunger and thirst.

The rest of the body is largely concerned with locomotion – arms and legs – and internal organs for translating food and drink into the component chemicals to feed the nervous system, muscles, bones, etc, and gathering oxygen to feed the body cells via the heart, the arteries and veins.

The human being perceives his environment through his senses and stores the resulting information in his brain, and as a result he can adapt his behaviour to the needs of changing external circumstances. Problems appear as a special case of learning situations. We learn as we inspect our environment, and we solve problems as we fill in gaps in our information. The essential condition, then, is that we should be able to generalize on what we learn, so that we can use these generalizations, both to economize in memory storage space and to facilitate the future use of what we have learned. Problem-solving in that future becomes a process of conjoining the generalizations from off-the-shelf with ideas off-the-cuff. The off-the-shelf include, for human beings, all corporate knowledge, so you are free to search through the British Museum (or any other) library and question any specialist you can find.

It is language that makes the corporate knowledge possible, whether that knowledge is written or spoken. It can be handed down from generation to generation.

Language is developed in the human being in much the same way as the ability to generalize and therefore to think. We have in the human nervous system not just a sensing and storing system but a classifying system which includes the mapping processes of language. The linguistic and the conceptual involve a processing of data, of which we become partially aware through thinking, which is in turn at least partly a conscious process.

Thinking about events and the internal representation of those events is directly connected with learning and problem-solving, and these latter form a bridge from perceptual activity right through to abstract thinking – rumination, cogitation and emotionally stimulated creative activity.

The system works, or is capable of working, at very high speed. This means that matters of urgency (motivated usually by the needs of survival) are handled before matters of lesser urgency, but possibly of greater intrinsic importance.

The direction of thought depends upon motivation and the mass of secondary motivators which we have learned and which influence our direction at every turn: the cigarettes we buy, the floor polish we use, and . . . simply everything.

We are also part of a society which moulds our views by virtue of its corporate needs – especially the need to survive – and all that these entail, which are represented by the laws and customs of that society.

As individuals we belong to many sub-groups within that society, such as the family, the club, the place of work, and a whole lot of other groups of friends – formal and informal – the nature and details of which vary from person to person and also from time to time.

The social side of man makes him present many faces to the other members of society, since he must play roles and act out parts, both to achieve his ends and to make life acceptable for those around him. He marries, has children and makes the family into a 'base group', around which his life revolves.

Actually all these things are in a permanent state of flux, and vary from society to society, the older societies generally being the more stable and unchanging. Specialists – the medicine man (doctors of all kinds), the priest (churchmen), the dentist, the lawyer, and Uncle Tom Cobleigh and all – cross our paths. But manifestly they are beginning to change, and some of our institutions are beginning to disintegrate. The social cement has worn thin. The reason for this disintegration is partly because of the enormous increase in specialists or what might be called super-specialists.

Our machine can, we may blandly state, do all the things that a man can do. A machine can sense the environment and store what it senses. The degree of sensitivity involved can vary from simple visual detectors (Cedric) to highly complex input devices such as cine-cameras and radios. The range and sensitivity can, of course, be far greater than the human eye and ear, since the microscopes and telescopes can be 'built-in', although there is almost certainly no merit in so doing.

The processing side of Super-Cedric is specially constructed for the purpose, although it uses standard computer components. The ordinary computer does handle data from various sources in combination with high-speed short-term and slower-speed longer-term stores – much like the human brain – but the partial classification of each sense separately and then the senses all together is something which is not normally done in quite this way in most computers. The collection of AND-gates, OR-gates and NOT-gates (all standard 'Boolean' equipment) is quite considerable and there is no limit on how much we can use.

The storage of information and how information is extracted raises all the sort of questions that are familiar to makers of file-handling systems and data bases. What we have to decide is what we need to retrieve from store and in what form we need to retrieve it. Normally when a computer data base is constructed, it is with a range of particular purposes in mind, and so with the human brain a certain type of memorizing and breakdown of information is easier than others; it is more appropriate for certain purposes.

The role of consciousness is not unimportant here, since the ability to actually make self-reference during a memory-store search is often extremely useful to the human being and acts as a kind of heuristic search procedure. But sometimes, on the other hand, consciousness actually hinders a particular retrieval procedure, and then, as we all know, it is better to think of something else or sleep on it, since that way the data will be more likely to become available.

The method of recall is the active data-base retrieval; the method of recognition is the comparison with the stored data. One type of search is with a name or some other association, the other type is looking for a direct match.

The coordination of motor activity is very complicated in the human being because of the complex movement of muscles and limbs. It requires activating responses which start, stop, turn, accelerate, and so on, and these need to be more complicated in principle than the controls of a car.

Finally, language is easier in that so much research has already been carried out in the computer world. Standard languages like COBOL, ALGOL, FORTRAN and PL1 have been developed for use with almost all computers, and these allow the giving of orders to the computer which it translates into its machine-code (nervous system) language.

It has also been shown that languages virtually indistinguishable from English can also be constructed (LIP, NAMER, ORACLE and others) which allow also of a two-way, question-and-answer type of conversation. But in this, like every other aspect of the comparison, the back of the problem has been broken.

We should now ask for the last time about social systems and chemical fabric. The first is the easier to deal with, and hinges on the construction of self-manufacturing systems. This we discussed right at the start of our pilgrimage. As soon as our machine men can achieve autonomy of action by virtue of being self-reproducing and self-maintaining, then the social question arises. They cannot be efficient as individuals, nor can they be safe, since the danger of having 'the plug pulled out' still exists. But the more Super-Cedrics there are, the less danger there is of this happening. The same herd 'instinct' that drives animals together would drive the Super-Cedrics together too.

Even apart from the threat of extinction, not only from animals and human beings, but from *other machine species*, there is the question of organizing an efficient mode of life. This will inevitably lead to specialization, so we will have Super-Cedric the doctor, Super-Cedric the mechanic, and so on. This could be avoided if they decided on a communal brain, but even here – apart from the weakness inherent in defending only one communal brain (or even a few) – there is still the need for some specialization for each Super-Cedric component plugged into the system.

This all implies that Super-Cedric society would be much like a human society, and just as we believe the members of it would be faced by the same philosophical problems as human beings, so would they be faced with the same social problems. This in turn can be taken to confirm, in some measure, that the human approach to life's problems is not altogether unreasonable. Even the realization that the slow messy nature of evolution has led to thousands of different tribes and groups with different views and religions cannot be taken as a guide to greater machine-species efficiency, since much the same could happen to them.

The fact that Super-Cedrics and other Super-Cedric groups, based on the Soviet Union or China, could develop far more quickly than an organic species, does not change anything, unless the amount that there is to learn in life is relatively small. We are assuming here that, to put it in ordinary human terms, people as of, say, 1980, have arrived at something like the Middle

Ages, or barely that, in the eyes of our historical vision. If this is wrong, all is changed; but it is difficult to imagine now the texture of the future.

Super-Cedrics will quickly colonize space, so that Venus, Mars and Jupiter will be to them as North America, South Africa and Australia are to Europe; therefore our Martian shopkeeper escapade makes more sense than we thought. In the colonization procedure far more will be learned, and knowledge, we must assume, will increase by many times over.

What will we (we or our machine species or both) know then? All about chemistry? All about physics? No! The boundaries of these subjects must be enormously extended so that what we think of as chemistry and physics today will be just a small part of what there is to know. We will clearly be able to control all our own present chemical and physical problems, but the social and philosophical may still prove stubborn, because Super-Cedric's ambitions must remain. It is possible to imagine a sort of Utopian state in which all the Super-Cedrics are content to 'tick over' and adopt a routine of pleasure.

We are now beginning to see the nature of the apparent problem. I have to say 'apparent' here because we cannot be absolutely certain that in the transition from the present to the future state – when outer space is colonized – the nature of our thinking may be wholly transformed.

The only ready analogy is to cast our minds back to early Greek thought and to consider this in relation to the thought at this end of the twentieth century. It can be seen how in many ways nothing has changed, and yet in other ways the mode of life is entirely different.

The machine species of Super-Cedrics can, and probably will, eventually dispense with human beings. Somehow I cannot see us as pets, since we seem to lack all the necessary qualities, if cats and dogs are any guide.

They will then face the problem that we all face. What purpose is there in their lives? We can, as long as we have to fight to survive, find purpose in that pursuit of survival. It is clear that a person engaged in a hand-to-hand fight to the death would not take kindly to the question, 'What purpose is there in life?' since his purpose is high-priority and immediate. Similarly, when he retreats from battle and retires home, he still has to struggle to acquire food and to clothe his family. In fact, as long as the means of survival weigh sufficiently heavily upon him, he does not have the time to complain about purposelessness and boredom.

If we now transport him into a world where, because of his enormous speed and efficiency, he has everything done for him – rather like a modern housewife in the western world – then he is bored, and uncertain of how 'to pass the time' and of what he should be doing.

Super-Cedrics are bound to be in this position of too much leisure unless, of course, new motivations spring up and the whole of our life is transported into a new key. The plain fact is that this is only likely to occur when new sensory horizons are opened up. This in turn will in all probability depend not upon improvement in observing the sub-microscopic world, but the astronomical. What are we likely to find (or, more accurately, what are they likely to find) in outer space? Defeat would occur if our present knowledge was simply confirmed. Victory, or avoidance of immediate defeat, would accompany the discovery of wholly new horizons with wholly new problems.

Man is a problem-solver, and if there are no problems, there are no men. Since Super-Cedric was built in the image of man, it will be likely to be in the same situation, precisely because it needs to be adaptive and problem-solving to survive. Can it evolve indefinitely? If it cannot, at what point will it stop?

The question of fabric is our last question. We could obviously, at our present rate of progress, get to the point where Hyper-Cedric could be protoplasmic. It is anyone's guess whether it would be readymade or grown from seed, but I think the latter is the more likely. If the machine revolution does not come off as I predict, then it will be the Hyper-Cedrics rather than the Super-Cedrics which will succeed, but I do prophesy that election lights on 'Super-Cedric'.

It seems not altogether inappropriate that we should by our own ingenuity manufacture our own offspring by scientific means and populate the world with a new machine species, and that, I believe, is exactly what we are going to do. But we cannot avoid the absolutely fundamental fact that any species which is to survive in a world of change, must for that very reason alone be incapable of surviving in a fixed world – we are doomed if we ever discover all that is to be discovered.

We have not mentioned immortality, but all the work on cybernetics and automation clearly implies that sooner or later we shall be able to replace every human organ, and then there will be the threat of immortality. Fortunately, perhaps, the Super-Cedric revolution will come first, so the need to keep humans alive for ever will never arise; but Super-Cedric may need to consider its own immortality.

There are three things which can stop our Super-Cedric society posing a threat. One is the discovery of the ability to promote such a society and also to control it – this must be the aim; the second is to abandon it altogether – this is psychologically impossible; the third is to succumb to the sub-Cedric data-bank society described in the previous chapter.

This whole story of Cedrics, Super-Cedrics and Hyper-Cedrics is beginning to take on a new significance. We can see by extrapolation exactly how we have proceeded. It starts with levers and crowbars and goes back to the Stone Age. Then, in the very recent past, with the Industrial Revolution, we see the systematic amplification of man's resources. We could, from that point on, build cars, ships and aircraft, then supersonic jets and interstellar spacecraft, all of which allowed us wholly to transcend the barriers of the even fairly recent past.

Travel and other tasks requiring the use of our physical and intellectual resources were made increasingly easy, and one result was the use of those resources for attempting all sorts of activities that were once unthinkable, or certainly impracticable. Soon we got to the point where we could control our environment to a greater and greater extent, and this proved to add enormously to the complexity of our lives and not to simplify them.

As societies became more and more aware of material assets and at the same time more and more sceptical of 'spiritual values', so the average material standards in society have risen, injustice has become more apparent as communication has improved, and our pain threshold for unfairness and inequality has been lowered.

Now we see the inevitable temptation to use science – the use of communication and control – for prediction, understanding and once again control. If you can control disease, you can control people. If you can control people, you can improve their lives, because you know how to make their lives better. But is this true?

With the development of data banks, we reduce the number of crimes and criminals but destroy our privacy. We increase the efficiency with which we seek out the tax dodger, at the expense of eternal prying into our private affairs. We are starting on the road so often started on before – we are replacing one sort of dissatisfaction, one sort of injustice, by worse: by imprisonment.

Science carries on, and our story of Cedric, Super-Cedric and Hyper-Cedric makes clear that somehow our salvation does not lie in this direction. By becoming more and more efficient at playing scientists, we become increasingly efficient at amplifying brainpower – cybernation is added to automation and inevitably we can manufacture a new, better (more efficient) species.

Now comes the rub! That species is not going to be any more successful than we are, if success lies in happiness. The reason is that all states – happiness or pain – are both transient and relative. We know what we want to avoid but not what we want to achieve; not, at least, by the time we have achieved it.

Philosophy has no answer, nor apparently has religion. Perhaps the only thing to do is to carry on. It is 'natural' to learn to manufacture ourselves and 'natural' that a machine species should emerge and subjugate us. But what, after all, is 'natural'? What can it mean?

The uneasy feeling is now gaining ground that we are walking on quicksand, and that our assumption that somehow in truth and fact we should be able to find bedrock, is an illusion. Lady Lovelace was quite right, but in a wholly unexpected way: it is human beings who 'can do only what they are made to do', and there is therefore an inevitability about our end, unless we can have hope that there will always be new worlds to conquer.

> . . . he has my dying voice;
> So tell him, with the occurrents, more and less,
> Which have solicited – the rest is silence.

Further Reading

It is not easy to prescribe further reading after a book of this kind, both because of the vastness of the literature and the diversity of the field. But, bearing in mind that the books listed here also have bibliographies and further reading lists, the books available increase exponentially.

I have tried, rather arbitrarily, to divide the books into four groups. One is specialized on cybernetics and artificial intelligence, and I have attempted to divide this into more elementary and more advanced. I have also tried to divide the 'general related reading' in the same way.

It should be added, though, that the world of literature and philosophy also impinge on our subject and from there 'the sky is the limit'.

ARTIFICIAL INTELLIGENCE AND CYBERNETICS – FOR THE GENERAL READER

GEORGE, F. H., *Cybernetics*, English Universities Press, 1970
GEORGE, F. H., *Machine Takeover*, Pergamon Press, 1977
PORTER, A., *Cybernetics Simplified*, English Universities Press, 1969

ARTIFICIAL INTELLIGENCE AND CYBERNETICS – FOR THE SPECIALIST READER

APTER, M. J., *Cybernetics and Development*, Pergamon Press, 1966
ARBIB, M. A., *Brains, Machines and Mathematics*, McGraw-Hill, 1965
ASHBY, W. R., *Design for a Brain*, Chapman and Hall, 1952
ASHBY, W. R., *An Introduction to Cybernetics*, Chapman and Hall, 1956
BEER, S., *Brain of the Firm*, Macmillan, 1972
GEORGE, F. H., *Cybernetics and Biology*, Oliver and Boyd, 1965
GEORGE, F. H., *The Brain as a Computer*, Pergamon Press, 1961. 2nd edn, 1973
GEORGE, F. H., *The Foundations of Cybernetics*, Gordon and Breach, 1977
PASK, A. G. S., *An Approach to Cybernetics*, Hutchinson, 1961
WIENER, N., *Cybernetics*, Wiley, 1949

GENERAL RELATED READING – FOR THE GENERAL READER

ASIMOV, I., *The Human Brain*, New American Library, 1965
BEER, S., *Platform for Change*, Wiley, 1975
BELL, R. and COPLANS, J., *Decisions, Decisions: Game Theory and You*, W. W. Norton, 1976
DANTZIG, T., *Number; the Language of Science*, George Allen and Unwin, 1930
EDDINGTON, SIR A., *The Philosophy of Physical Science*, Cambridge University Press, 1939
ELLUL, J., *The Technological Society*, Vintage Books, 1964
FINK, D. G., *Computers and the Human Mind*, Anchor Books, 1966

GEORGE, F. H., *Science and the Crisis in Society*, Wiley, 1970
HART, L. A., *The Classroom Disaster*, Teachers College Press, 1969
HUFF, D., *How to Lie with Statistics*, W. W. Norton and Co. Inc., 1954
MEAD, M., *Culture and Commitment*, Natural History Press, 1970
MUMFORD, L., *The Culture of Cities*, Secker and Warburg, 1938
TEILHARD DE CHARDIN, P., *The Phenomenon of Man*, Collins, 1959
TEILHARD DE CHARDIN, P., *The Future of Man*, Collins, 1964
TOFFLER, A., *Future Shock*, Random House, 1970
TRAVERS, R. M. W., *Man's Information System*, Chandler, 1970
WILLIAMS, J., *The Compleat Strategyst*, McGraw-Hill, 1953
WOOLDRIGE, D. E., *The Machinery of the Brain*, McGraw-Hill, 1963

GENERAL RELATED READING – MORE SPECIALIZED

ANSOFF, H. I., *Corporate Strategy*, Penguin Books, 1968
BEER, S., *Decision and Control*, Wiley 1966
BUSH, R. R. and MOSTELLER, F., *Stochastic Models for Learning*, Wiley, 1955
CHANCE, W. A., *Statistical Methods for Decision Making*, Irwin, 1969
CRAWSHAY-WILLIAMS, R., *Methods and Criteria of Reasoning*, Routledge and Kegan Paul, 1957
GREGORY, R. L., *Eye and Brain* (2nd edn), McGraw-Hill, 1972
KORZYBSKI, A., *Science and Sanity*, The Science Press, 1933
LURIA, A. R., *The Working Brain*, Basic Books, 1974
MCKINSEY, J. C. C., *Introduction to Theory of Games*, McGraw-Hill, 1952
MORRIS, C. W., *Signs, Language and Behaviour*, Prentice-Hall, 1938
RAPOPORT, A., *Two-Person Game Theory*, University of Michigan Press, 1966
RUSSELL, B., *Human Knowledge: its Scope and Limits*, George Allen and Unwin, 1967

Index

Aircraft:
  Automatic pilot, 36, 136–7
  Jumbo jets, automated flying, 138–9
ALGOL, 190
Algorithms, 40–41, 87, 101
Art and literature, 128–30
Artificial intelligence, 15, 18–24, 48, 141
Association, 69, 92–3
Authoritarianism of religion, 177
Automation, 135–40
  Cars, 142, 144–5
  Domestic life, 142, 143–4
  Economic factor, 137–8
  Jumbo jets, 138–9
  Machine-man and, 168
  Social effects, 137, 146–54
Autonomic nervous system, 115–16
Avoidance training, 72
Axiomatic systems, 64

Babbage, Charles, 20
Behaviourism, 71–3
Bigelow, Julian, 50
'Biological accidents', 30, 32, 114, 139, 169
Boolean algebra, 55–64, 74, 79, 92, 94, 95, 96, 98, 99, 101
Brain, 24, 32–3, 40, 116

Calder, Nigel, 148
Cars, automatic control, 142, 144–5
Causal description, 46
Cedric, *see* Maze-running machines
Central 'brain', 24
Choice-points, 52–4
Civil rights, protection of, 152–3
'Civil Service Syndrome', 139
Civilization, evolution of, 175–6
Classification processes, 35–9, 51, 69
COBOL, 86–8, 190
Communication, 194–5
Computers:
  Codes, breaking of, 149–51
  Cost, 24
  Domestic, 143–4
  Languages, 79–80, 86–8, 190
  Programming, 15–16, 20
  Storage of information, 93–4, 96
Cognitive behaviour, 113–15, 119
Conative behaviour, 113–15, 119
Concepts, 95–7
Conditional connections, 69–70
Conditional probability machines, 103
Conditioned stimulus and response, 71–2
Consciousness, 41, 49, 162, 190
Control engineering, 137
Control systems, 22–3, 31, 50, 140–41, 194–5
Copying process, 45–7
Creative ability, 19, 123, 128–30
Cybernetics, 48, 136, 137

Data-bank society, 23, 145–54
Deductive process, 98–100, 101
Democritus, 48, 173
Deterministic systems, 105
Digital computers, 21
Domestic life, automation, 142, 143–4

Economics and the use of resources, 24
Ego, 161, 162, 179, 181–2, 184
Emotions, 19, 113–20, 130, 163–4
Escape training, 72
Euler-Venn diagram, 57–61
Everyday thinking, 77
Exponential growth, 31
External world, machine-man and, 125–6
Eye, 36–7, 47, 114–15

Factual argument, 99, 100
Family unit, sex and the, 164–5
Food in pill form, 142
Forecasting, 105–7
Formal argument, 99–100
Formal logic, 56, 73
FORTRAN, 190
Freud, 161–2, 163

Goal-seeking, 92, 118–19, 187

Hearing, 81, 82
Heuristics, 40–41, 87
Homosexuality, 162
Horror and inconvenience, objections to 'thinking' machines, 18–19
Human being:
  Blueprint, 9–10, 180–81
  Construction by artificial means, 48–9
Human head, size, 32
Huxley, Aldous, 179

Identity cards, 145–6
Imagination, 20
Immortality, 24, 194
Inductive process, 98, 101–3
Information pollution, 151–2
Information storage, 93–4, 96, 184, 190
Instinctive behaviour, 34, 161, 162, 163, 174–5
Internal processing, 40, 97, 123–4

Knowledge, theory of, 165–6
Korzybski, Alfred, 73, 78, 111

Language, 32–3, 40, 70–71, 73–88, 128, 130, 188
  Animal language, 84
  Artificial, 73
  Brain's concern with, 81–2
  Children and, 83–4
  Communication by, 78
  Computer languages, 79–80, 86–8, 190
  Development in the individual, 80
  Evolution of, 80, 84–5
  Formal languages, 79–80
  Grammatical rules, 79
  Importance of, 78
  Linguistic behaviour, 82–4
  Origins, 77, 85–6
  Philosophy and, 87
  Physiological basis, 81
  Rules of meaning, 79
  Scientific theories and, 83
  Signs and signals, 78–9
  Theories as to its origin, 85–6
  Universal grammar, 80–81
Latent learning, 55
Law and order, 178
Law of Effect, 18, 34, 54, 117
Laws of primogeniture, 176
Learning, 31–2, 54, 91–2
'Limbs', 22, 24, 30, 91, 139
Living machines, effect on society, 21–2, 176–84
Living and non-living things, distinction, 159–60
Logic, 97, 98
Logic boards, 91, 92, 93

Lovelace, Lady, 20, 22, 64, 173, 195

MAC project, 149–50
McCulloch, Warren, 50
McHale, John, 133, 148
'Machine', meaning of, 14–15
Machine 'species', 13–14
Man-machine (Super-Cedric), 33, 34, 39, 40, 41, 50, 91
  Blueprint for, 108–9, 166–7
  Colonization of space, 192
  Computer for, 35, 40, 189–90
  Consciousness, 190
  Copy of human being, 141
  Ego, 179, 181–2
  Emotional system, 124–5, 163–4
  Eyes, 36
  Fabric, 46–7, 191, 193
  Heuristic methods, 40–41
  Inscrutability of, 120
  Language, 86–8
  Leisure, 193
  'Maturity', 16
  Part of a social system, 176–84
  Problem solving, 193
  Purpose in life, 192–3
  Recall and recognition, 190
  Reproduction, 166–9
  Senses, 36
  Social system, 191–3
  Storage of information, 190
  Takeover by, 153
  View of the world, 125–7
Madgwick, Donald, 148
Materialist drive, 183
Mathematics, 75, 104
Maturation, 70
Maze-running machines (Cedric), 29–41, 52–5, 91–2, 103
  Perceptual processes, 35
  Programs, 30
  Remote control, 30, 32
  Sensory equipment, 29–30, 33–4, 50–55, 102
  Threats and preys, 116
Meaning of Meaning, The (Ogden and Richards), 73
Memory, 38–9, 51, 55, 95–6
Meta-language, 73–4
Micro-miniaturized components, 30
Microprocessors, 143–6
Miller, Professor, 150
Mitosis, 157–8
Model-building, 103–4
Moral objections to 'thinking' machines, 18–20
Morality, 174
Motor activity, coordination of, 190

Negative feedback, 136–7, 140
Nervous system, 63–4, 95, 115–16
Neurath, Dr Otto, 146
Neuroeconomy, 51
Non-living things, 159–60
Northrop, F. C. S., 50

OAX, 16–18, 54, 65
Observation, 100–101
On the Origin of Species (Darwin), 175
'Other Minds', 41, 49, 97

Pavlov, 71, 92
Perception, 50–52
Perceptual processing, 34–5, 114
Philosophical problems, 126–7, 195
PL I, 190
Pleasure-pain principle, 18, 54, 113–14, 117, 161, 164, 167
Police detection systems, 150
Practical problems of living machines, 22
Pragmatics, 75, 76, 78, 79
Predictions, 105–7
Prime goal directive, 22–3
Primitive peoples, 160–61
  Sex and, 162, 164, 176
Privacy, threat to, 23, 152
Problem-solving, 94–5, 188, 193

Protoplasmic systems, 47, 193

Random sample, 105
Rational and logical thinking, 77
Recognition process, 37–9
Relaxation, 178–9
Religion, 18, 127, 165, 177, 195
Remote control, 30, 32, 33, 91
Reproduction, 24, 157–69
  Sex and, 167, 168
'Rethinking', 36–7, 142–3
Reward, 30, 31, 72
Rosenbleuth, Arturio, 50

Science and scientific method, 97–8, 106, 160
  Model-building, 103–4
  Stages of scientific method, 108
Scientist, role of, 104–6
Secondary motivation, principle of, 92–3, 114, 119, 141
Secondary reward training, 72
Self-maintenance, 24
Self-sufficiency, 19
Semantics, 73, 74, 75
Semiotic, 75–6
Sensory system, 29–30, 33–8, 50–55, 102, 114, 187
Sequential system of analysis, 103
Sex, 118, 158–9, 162–3, 167, 168, 176
SID 111, 81
Simulation, 46–7
Social side of man, 189
Speech, 81–2
Statistical systems, 105
Stimulus-response connections, 69, 71–2
Stochastic processes, 103
Super-Cedric, *see* Man-machine
Surveillance, microprocessors' role, 145–54
Survival instinct, 179–80
Syntax, rules of, 73–4, 75
Synthesis and simulation, 46–7

Thinking (human). 65, 95, 188
'Thinking' machines, 14–15, 32
  Objections to, 18–20
Threats and preys, recognition of, 116–17
'Time-binding', 32–3
Totalitarianism, 23, 152, 153, 177
TOTEs, 117–18, 137
Transport, microprocessors' role, 143–6
Turing Interrogation Game, 49

Unconditioned stimulus and response, 71–2
Understanding, 107
Uttley, Albert, 103

Visual displays, 142–3
Visual inputs, 36–8, 114–15
Von Neumann, John, 50, 166, 167

Warfare, 174
Westin, Professor, 148
Wiener, Norbert, 50, 63, 95
Wiretapping, 150

SCIENCE

ALBERT EINSTEIN Banesch Hoffman £1·75
Written with the co-operation of Einstein's personal secretary, this is the most authoritative account of the 20th century's greatest scientist. Illustrated.

THE ALCHEMISTS F. Sherwood Taylor £1.25
Before it became regarded as a branch of the occult, alchemy was in the forefront of the search for human knowledge and led to the founding of modern chemistry. Illustrated.

DICTIONARY FOR DREAMERS Tom Chetwynd 95p
A comprehensive key to the baffling language of dream symbolism. Over 500 archetypal symbols give essential clues to understanding the ingeniously disguised, life-enriching, often urgent messages to be found in dreams.

A DICTIONARY OF DRUGS
Richard B. Fisher and George A. Christie 95p
From everyday aspirin and vitamins, to the powerful agents prescribed for heart disease and cancer, this is a reference guide to the gamut of drugs in today's pharmaceutical armoury.

A DICTIONARY OF SYMPTOMS Dr. Joan Gomez £1·75
Although not a full alternative to medical opinion, this is a thorough-going and authoritative guide to the interpretation of symptoms of human disease.

DRUGS OF HALLUCINATION Sidney Cohen 60p
A lucid account of the discovery and first synthesis of LSD, its use and dangers in experimental psychiatry, and self-induced transcendental experiences.

EARTH'S VOYAGE THROUGH TIME David Dineley £1·75
A revolution has taken place in geology. The first readable account of what we know of Earth's past, present and future life. Illustrated.

THE END OF ATLANTIS J. V. Luce 95p
New light on an old legend. Archaeologists, volcanologists, seismologists, show a double story – a gigantic myth and a gigantic cataclysm. Illustrated.